# ON LOVE

BENEDICT XVI
JOSEPH RATZINGER

# ON LOVE

*Selected Writings*

*Edited by*
Pierluca Azzaro

*Translated by*
Michael J. Miller

IGNATIUS PRESS    SAN FRANCISCO

Cover design by Roxanne Mei Lum

# CONTENTS

## ADVENT AND THE CHRISTMAS SEASON

*Someone Who Has Found Love Can Say:*
*I Have Found Life*                                     9

*Only Love Knows Love*                                 14

*How God Comforts*                                     18

*God's Weeping and the Promise of Victory*             23

*Mary's Yes: "Blessed Is She Who Believed"*            31

*Plunging into God's Love*                             35

## LENT AND THE EASTER SEASON

*The Celebration of Lent*                              43

*"Behold Your Mother!" These Words Are*
*Addressed to Us, Too*                                 47

*Joseph's Faith*                                       52

*"Do with Me What You Will, Only Grant*
*That I May Love You Completely"*                      57

*When God Kneels Down before Us*                       63

*"I Have Risen, and Now I Am Always with You"*         69

# ORDINARY TIME

*"Blessed Are You When Men Hate You"*     79

*When a Machine Is Blessed*     86

*"Only He Who Experiences the Absurd Is Able to Conquer the Impossible" (Miguel de Unamuno)*     89

*On the Way to the Land of the Future*     96

*Jesus and the Faith of the Little Ones*     102

*The Genuine Miracle Is God Crucified*     110

*The Main Thing Needed to Purify the Empoisoned Air of This World*     118

*The Cross: The Love That Gives Itself, Total Self-Giving to Others*     123

*The Sign of Mary*     128

*The Fair, Good Heart of Mary*     135

*Believe, and You Will See . . .*     141

*All Saints: The Feast That Drives Away Despair*     147

Sources     151

Index     155

# ADVENT AND
# THE CHRISTMAS SEASON

# SOMEONE WHO HAS FOUND LOVE CAN SAY: I HAVE FOUND LIFE

*1 Jn 3:11–24; Deut 30:15–20*

"We know that we have passed out of death into life" (1 Jn 3:14). With these words, Saint John explains the essence of Christianity. Being Christian is a passage from death to life. Christianity is therefore a movement, a journey; it is not a theory, a sum total of doctrine; Christianity is life, it is a vital impetus that carries us toward true life and thus also opens our eyes to the truth, which is not pure thought but, rather, is a creative force fundamentally identical to charity.

"We know that we have passed out of death into life." Christianity is therefore the inversion of the normal direction of our existence. Human life, according to its natural tendency, is a journey toward death. The process of life is in itself a progress toward death, toward the dissolution of this wonderful synthesis that is life. Probably Saint John, with his definition of Christian existence, not only means to point out the inversion of the normal tendency of all life in the new baptismal process, but is also alluding to the origin of human history. The first man, according to God's design, begins his existence in paradise, that is, in closeness to God, in fraternal friendship with all creatures, in perfect correspondence with the woman and thus in security unclouded by fear and in a wealth that depends, not on having great material possessions, but rather on the profound harmony of all creatures among themselves and with their Creator. This unlimited life ends and changes into a process leading to death at the moment when man tries to emancipate himself from divine love, to make himself independent of God through his own knowledge of the mysteries of being. We could say in a word: the first sin was the passage from love to covetousness; thus man passes from life to non-life, from true life to a life that is an advance toward death. Gone is the security offered by closeness to God, by fraternity with creatures; gone is the wealth bestowed in the harmony of creation; gone is the joy of love that, forgetting self, receives all the beauty of the world as a gift. Gone, therefore, is paradise, and now a world full of dangers and threats appears.

"We know that we have passed out of death into life." Now we can answer the question raised by these words: What is life? When can someone say: "I have found life"? Where do we find it? Let us listen now to the whole verse by the apostle and we will have the answer: "We know that we have passed out of death into life, because we love the brethren." Love is life. Love is synthesis; death is dissolution. Someone who has found love can say: I have found life. The inversion of the process of death in a passage to life occurs in the conversion from covetousness to love. Christianity is conversion to divine love and, thus, to fraternal love and, hence, a passage from death to life.

Christianity is opting for life against the dominion of death. All the commandments of God are nothing other than elaborations of this fundamental option. The Mosaic Law comes at the end of the long journey in the desert, at the gates of the Promised Land, summed up in the words: "See, I have set before you this day life and good, death and evil.... I call heaven and earth to witness against you this day, that I have set before you life and death, blessing and curse; therefore choose life,... loving the LORD your God ...; for that means life to you" (Deut 30:15, 19–20). The criterion of the judgment, therefore, as we see today in the Gospel, is love that awards life to the other and, thus, opposes the dominion of death. The judge's decision, by which some will go to eternal torment and others to eternal life, is not a positivist condemnation or an external prize; this decision merely reveals what the profound reality of a human life is: some are servants of death, closed in on themselves; in their exclusive search for their own independence and their own will, they are opposed to reciprocal dependence, which in the relation of love becomes the wonderful synthesis of life and freedom. Others, in contrast, by losing themselves give life in the act of love, and thus the whole movement of their being is a walk toward life.

"Truly, I say to you, as you did it to one of the least of these my brethren, you did it to me" (Mt 25:40). These words of the judge of the world—the Son of God—have acquired today a current relevance that was still unforeseeable not long ago. The helpless least ones, the closest brethren of the Lord today, are the children who are not yet born, and tomorrow perhaps they will be also the elderly and the sick who no longer participate in the process of production. Recently an Australian researcher was asked by a member of Parliament whether, instead of performing his experiments on human fetuses, it would be possible to use the fetuses of the apes that are closest to human beings. The scientist's answer was that these species would be too valuable to be used in such experiments, while—he said—we have more than enough fetuses of the human species. Science, which originated to defend life, thus becomes an instrument of death like the autonomous knowledge of Adam that destroyed paradise. In drafting our document on life (the CDF Instruction on Respect for Human Life in its Origin and on the Dignity of Procreation, *Donum vitae*, February 22, 1987), I increasingly realized, to my great surprise, that this text is nothing but a concrete application of our principles concerning freedom and liberation, of the principle of the preferential option for the poor. Where unconditional respect for the weak, the defenseless, and the helpless no longer rules, we are in a regime of violence where law is replaced by violence. And where violence dominates, we are in the dominion of death.

"We know that we have passed out of death into life, because we love the brethren." We can also turn these words around: Only by loving the brethren do we pass from death into life. And only this passage is the redemption of the world. The saints help us to live out these words, to love "not ... in word or speech but in deed and in truth" (1 Jn 3:18). The lives of the saints are the authentic interpretation of Scripture. Today the debate among theologians has become public; in the mass media, they talk about persons who are competent or incompetent to speak about the problems of Christian life, and in this terrible turmoil the faithful wonder: But how can we find a sure orientation again? Here it is: the lives of the saints are the great beacon that shows us where to go, in the darkness of the debates. The Collect prayer for the Feast of Blessed Luigi Orione, a priest, sums up the essence of his life by saying that this man made the brethren "experience the tenderness of [God's] Fatherly love". Quite a different sort of "experiment" compared to the lethal experiments of the Australian scientist of whom we spoke a moment ago! In light of this great figure, we can understand also that the option for life—that is, the preferential option for the forgotten, the orphans, the handicapped, the elderly—and deciding in favor of God's love are inseparable. Where love for God is extinguished, human love becomes egotistical, and egotism is always an option against life. Therefore, true fraternal love can never limit itself to the protection of biological life or to structural, social liberation, but awards to the other also the more substantial and more fundamental gift of human life: the love and the knowledge of God.

Let us pray that the Lord may help us to "make the brethren experience the tenderness of [His] Fatherly love".

# ONLY LOVE KNOWS LOVE

*Eph 1:3–6, 11–12; Lk 1:26–38*

The reading from the Letter of Saint Paul to the Ephesians appears to be a description of the mystery of the Immaculate Conception of Mary: "[Chosen] in him before the foundation of the world, that [she] should be holy and blameless before him ... in love" (compare Eph 1:4–5). Of course this passage as such speaks about common Christian life, about our mystery, but it occurs totally and in an exemplary way only in the first chosen woman, who is the Daughter of Zion, the Church in person, the perfect model of Christian existence. Mary's election does not separate her from us, shutting her off in a sphere that is inaccessible to us; on the contrary, in the mirror of her exemplary vocation, we can learn the mystery of our own life. In her and from her we can see and understand what grace is, what freedom and a life in communion with Christ are. The core of the mystery of the Immaculata is thus explained with three concepts:

holy and immaculate
before him (i.e., in God's sight)
in love.

The content of these three phrases is disclosed if we begin our reading with the third element: "in love". Living in grace is the equivalent of being in charity. Grace is the Holy Spirit, or, in other words: grace is charity. Grace is not something in our soul; grace is essentially relation, it is the opening of the soul to its true destiny, to the love of God. Being in grace means: letting oneself be permeated by the divine love and to become a lover in the totality of our existence.

In this way, we understand the second note from our reading: "in his sight". God is love, and only love can perceive the divine reality. Knowledge always presupposes a certain equality or at least analogy between the knower and the thing known. Hatred or a cold mentality cannot know substantial love: God. Only love knows love. Therefore, divine knowledge begins with the initiative of divine love for us and is accomplished if we accept the offering of his love. Thus, we enter into a wonderful circle of knowledge and love. Love makes us see, and seeing makes us love. All this becomes concrete in our Lady: Mary lives in God's sight, in his presence. The glance of her heart is always fixed on God, and in the divine light, she does see correctly his creatures, also. By looking at God, she learns love, becomes love. By looking at God, she enters into her own truth, because our truth is that God's eyes are always upon us. And thus Mary becomes glad and free, free from fear. The core of all fear is the fear of loneliness, the fear of being unloved. Therefore Saint John says: "There is no fear in love, but perfect love casts out fear" (1 Jn 4:18).

In saying this, we have already interpreted the first Marian expression in our reading: "holy and blameless" or "immaculate". The word "holy" describes the divine sphere, the property of the divine being. To be holy, applied to a creature, means that he continually lives in relation to the divine being, "partakes in the divine nature" (see 2 Pet 1:4). To be immaculate means to be free from alienating factors that are incompatible with our essence, which is being in the image and likeness of God, and not falling here and there into dissimilarity. Or, in other words: to be holy and blameless means to live in the word of the Lord: "You, therefore, must be perfect, as your heavenly Father is perfect" (Mt 5:48). And in what other way can we be "like the Father" if not by being like the Son, in union with the Son, Jesus Christ? This key word of the Sermon on the Mount conceals the mystery of the Body of Christ, which we are; it conceals the mystery that in the sacraments we can become one with Christ (see Gal 3:28). And who in the world was as united with Christ as his Mother was and is? Therefore, the words of today's reading apply here in a singular way: "[Chosen] before the foundation of the world ... to be holy and blameless".

With these reflections, we have also found the answer to an oft-recurring question: But are we still free if grace precedes us? Was Mary free, even though she was chosen to be immaculate before creation? Can Mary with her singular predestination be a model for us? Hidden behind these questions is a mistaken concept of freedom, a confusion between freedom and arbitrariness. To live in grace means to live in the original design of our being, to live in a way consistent with our truth, with the creative plan for our existence; to unite our Yes with God's Yes to us, thus entering into the unification of our lives with the divine life. Our fundamental error concerning freedom appears at this point. We always think that the core of freedom is the possibility to say No, and consequently that freedom is manifested in opposing another contrary will to the divine will, in creating a reality that is ours alone. The contrary is true. The fundamental word of freedom is Yes; No does not create but destroys. Things that are ours alone and opposed to God are opposed also to truth and to love. True creativity unfolds only in the immense space of the divine love. Certainly, grace demands of us the humility to accept the fact that God precedes us with his love; it demands obedience in accepting his plan of love. Only this Yes opens up the space of true freedom.

Grace is not opposed to freedom; on the contrary, freedom is a daughter of grace. A person who is always seeking himself thereby actually loses himself and loses everything. Only a person who opens himself, forgets himself, does not seek his own life but places himself fearlessly at the disposition of eternal love, finds himself along with God. The humble Virgin of Nazareth shows us the way: "Behold, I am the handmaid of the Lord; let it be to me according to your word" (Lk 1:38). With these words, she placed herself unreservedly into God's hands. And thus she obtained life for herself and for everyone. Let us follow her.

# HOW GOD COMFORTS

*Is 40:1–5, 9–11; Mk 1:1–8*

"Comfort, comfort my people!" (Is 40:1). We just heard the voice of the prophet Isaiah proclaim this, and these great, ancient words of hope and confidence of the people of Israel, which the Church presents to us in Advent, always touch our hearts anew. In the history of the prophets, this struck a new note. At first, in the time of the kings, the prophets—starting with Elijah and continuing through Amos, Hosea, and Micah, down to Isaiah and Jeremiah—had above all admonished harshly and demandingly; they stirred the conscience of the powerful and those who were self-assured in their external righteousness, and they stood up for the cause of the forgotten, the widows, the orphans, and the poor. Again and again, they spoke troubling, upsetting words like these: "I can no longer listen to your feasts and your prayers; I can no longer endure the smell of your incense. The fast that I want is, rather, to do justice to the orphan and the widow" (see Is 1:11–17).

At the end of this long series of stirring admonishers is Jeremiah, who takes a stance with the reasonableness of faith against the stubborn nationalism that tries to co-opt God and becomes a martyr. Next came the great silence of the Babylonian Exile. And now, after seventy years, after Israel has been crushed and seems almost extinct, this altogether new voice is heard!

Enough suffering. The major power that deported you no longer exists. The gates of the fatherland stand open.

The wilderness becomes a road, and now the downtrodden, the vanquished, are at last the true victors after all. God remembered them, and he is more powerful than the major powers of this world, even though he takes his time in history. "Comfort my people!" God does not forget the suffering but loves them and lifts them up.

As much as this moves us and touches our hearts, an objection or at least a question nevertheless remains in us. Is this consolation not too long ago? And did it not achieve much too little? Indeed, very soon Israel itself fell once more into disgrace. And if we look at the world today, we still see images of desolation that cause us concern.

Precisely when we see this, when we see how desolation dominates in the midst of well-to-do nations, we wonder all the more: "Lord, where is your consolation?" But perhaps we also understand all the more that we need the Church, which with full authority can proclaim today in the name of the Lord those words from back then: "Comfort my people!" She is the one who gives true consolation.

Over the course of her liturgical year, the Church runs again, so to speak, through the entire history of salvation. For many weeks, she appears before us with the demeanor of Hosea or Elijah: in other words, admonishing us, stirring us, exhorting us, trying to tear us away from our egotism, our greed, our self-complacency, just as the prophets did in that time. But in Advent, the good Lord's hour arrives, the time of the God who comforts. It becomes evident that the Church is not only a moral institution and that she does not just make demands, but that she is the grace-filled space in which God comes to meet her above all as the One who grants and gives.

But then the question arises: Where is this consolation? How does God comfort in reality? What has he really done? What does he really give us?

Now the first level consists of the fact that once again we are called. He wants us to let the light of faith that he put into our hearts shine forth and, thereby, warm the world. He wants to comfort through us, and he lets us know that he loves in a special way precisely the disconsolate, that he identifies with them and in them awaits us and our goodness.

The name of the Holy Spirit is "Consoler". The more we ourselves are people who console, people who show comforting goodness, the more God helps us in the Holy Spirit.

This means also that we must not be like those for whom the small consolation of everyday life is too little and who say: No, this system must be transformed; we need a world in which consolation is no longer necessary; or else, as Bertolt Brecht said, advancing the idea: "We want a world in which we no longer need love."

But a world like that, in which there is no longer any need for consolation, would be a desolate world; a world in which love is no longer necessary, because the system already provides for everything, would be an inhuman world. God wants to console through us.

But instead, there is still a gnawing suspicion that these are mere words, *empty* promises. Let us ask a very practical question: What happens when a man comforts a child whose mother has died? He cannot undo that death; he cannot remove the sorrow caused by it; he cannot magically transform the world with all its sadness. He can, however, enter into the loneliness left by the ruined love, which is the genuine reason for the sorrow, as someone who shares the sorrow and shares the love. Thus, although he cannot take back what has happened, he is not just all talk; rather, when he enters lovingly into the loneliness of the lost love, transforms it from within, he heals the essential thing. And it is quite clear: if he is truly compassionate and loving, then his words will not be just words.

God did not work—as we might dream and as Karl Marx then shouted at the top of his voice to the world—in such a way as to make sorrow vanish and to change the system, so that there is no longer any need for consolation. That would be to take away our humanity. And this is what we secretly desire. Yes, being human is too burdensome for us. But if our humanity were taken away from us, we would cease to be human beings and the world would become inhuman. God did not work that way. He chose a wiser way that was more difficult in many respects but, for precisely that reason, better, more divine. He did not take away our humanity but shares it with us. He entered into the loneliness of ruined love as one who shares the sorrow, as a consolation. This is the divine way of redemption. Maybe from this we can best understand what redemption means in the Christian sense: not a magical transformation of the world, not that our humanity is taken away from us, but that we are consoled, that God shares with us the burden of life, and that now the light of his compassionate love remains forever in our midst.

Isaiah had said: "In the wilderness prepare the way" (Is 40:3). John the Baptist knows that the hour of the great consolation has arrived, nevertheless, the lack of a way is not in fact exterior but above all interior. What separates human beings from each other are mountains that are found in the heart and that ought to melt away so that there might be a way. He calls for this, and besides this he announces the one who is the Way. When we allow him to enter, a human being is transformed from the foundations. Mountains and valleys that separate us disappear. He gives us the way to one another.

"Where art Thou, consolation of the whole world?" we sing in one of our beautiful German Christmas hymns taken from the Old Testament: *O Heiland, reiss den Himmel auf* [O Savior, rend open the heavens]. With these words (see Is 45:8), Israel stirred God's heart; with these words, we, too, stir his heart, so that he makes us experience his consolation. But with these words, he stirs us, too, so that we might be open, so that we might not aspire to a magically transformed world but might become sincere and human in his light and be open to the true consolation, let it enter into us, so that it can shine forth from us, so that the world might become an authentically Advent world, a comforted world.

Let us pray to him that this might happen, and in this Advent season let us set out on this way.

# GOD'S WEEPING AND THE
# PROMISE OF VICTORY

*Is 48:17–19; Mt 11:16–19*

The texts of today's liturgy, for Friday of the Second Week of Advent, are full of light for our journey and help us to realize the essence of expectation, which then is the essence of our being Christians.

I would like to begin with the prayer for the day: "Grant that your people, we pray, almighty God, may be ever watchful for the coming of your Only Begotten Son, that, as the author of our salvation himself has taught us, we may hasten, alert and with lighted lamps, to meet him when he comes."

The fundamental word of today's prayer is "watchful", which among other things is the key word of all Advent. Watchfulness, to be watchful: What does this mean?

Someone who sleeps is shut up in himself, does not perceive the reality outside him, and even in his dreams he is not capable of perceiving reality, but sees only the reflected shadows of his mind, of his subconscious. On awakening, he comes out of the prison, emerges from the walls of himself, and perceives the reality that surrounds him. He becomes open to it.

Our generation is convinced that it is really very "awake", more than all preceding generations, only because it manages to perceive much more of the world: our eyesight goes to the farthest distances, immense distances both in

23

space and in time. And at the same time, we are capable of entering also into the interior of matter, down to the smallest particles of which it is composed. The horizon has been broadened enormously and so have our possibilities of acting in this world.

And all this notwithstanding, we must say that this generation, in a much more profound sense, is asleep. It is shut up in itself, because it sees only what it can do and have, and it stops at the exterior face of reality, at the material things that it can take in hand.

But in precisely this way, we are increasingly self-enclosed, and we are no longer capable of really approaching the infinite, of seeing the transparency of the divine light in created matter, of looking into ourselves with the eye of our heart: our interior senses—overshadowed by seeing all these exterior things that help us to do and to have—no longer respond, no longer function, no longer have access to the true reality, to the greatness of the world. This is the reason why we sleep. Our generation is asleep.

Through his Advent, the Lord tells us to wake up, to come out of the prison of what is material, to open our hearts and to begin to see the greater reality, the Spirit of God in the world, the presence of God in the Lord Jesus Christ, in his Word, in his sacraments.

This is the first imperative that obliges us also to open the eyes of our hearts and to help our friends, our contemporaries, so that they can begin again to see the true profundity and the true greatness of reality. To see means also to be detached from oneself, and, thus, from the word "watchfulness" emerges the other expression characteristic of the Advent journey: "going to meet the Lord".

Faith is not a collection of ideas, but an adventure in life, a journey, setting out toward the Lord, and the exterior journey that we make in preparation for [World Youth

Day 2005 in] Cologne ought to be at the same time and above all an interior journey, a going out of ourselves so as to go to meet God, the true reality, love, and our neighbor.

Here we see, then, a third important word in this prayer, the Word of God, which is called "light", and the invitation to light the lamps of our being in order to arrive at the Lord. What does this mean?

If we look at the history of the Church, the history of the saints, we see these lighted "lamps" that illumine the world, and we see that they not only illuminate this era but will be decorations and lights in the eternal feast of God's love. We begin with the martyrs of the first century, and we continue with the great Doctors: Augustine, Ambrose, Bonaventure, Thomas, lighted lamps that illuminate and continue to illuminate the path of history. And then Saint Francis of Assisi, Saint Charles Borromeo, Saint Dominic, Saint Teresa of Ávila, Saint John of the Cross, Saint Thérèse of Lisieux, down to Maximilian Kolbe, Padre Pio, Edith Stein, Mother Teresa ...

Really, in the darkness of history—because it often is dark: think of the violence in this era, all the wars— there are lighted lamps that illumine, that make us see that there is light, that man is not an accident of creation but can be like God. They strengthen us along the path of love, because God is love. And we are like God in the measure in which we travel the path of love.

From the prayer for the day, let us move now to the Reading and the Gospel. The two are closely interconnected, and especially today we see, between the Reading and the Gospel, the close unity of the Old and the New Testament.

Both speak about God's suffering in relation to man, his creature. God suffers. Why does he not impose his way on his creature with the strength of his omnipotence?

Instead of doing that, he asks for his love, comes to meet our freedom, because he does not want to obtain anything by force, but desires love, unconditional love, and thus leaves us our freedom to say yes to his offering and to his invitation to love, or else to say no. Unfortunately, it happens that the creature man almost always says no and thinks that saying no is the only way to prove his freedom. God seeks man in every way possible; the Lord tells us this in today's Gospel with a parable. He seeks us on the path of strictness, of the Commandments, on Sinai, at the time of the prophets, in the words of John the Baptist. And man responds: "No, I am free, I do not accept the strictness of these commandments, I go my own way."

God seeks us also on the path of humility, of goodness, with his life, with love for mankind. And what happens? Here, too, man says no, and he even ridicules this weak God who seeks his consent and thus reveals that he is not omnipotent. In the Gospel, we read: "'We piped to you, and you did not dance; we wailed, and you did not mourn'" (Mt 11:17). Man does not enter into this dynamic of divine love; he opposes it. Hence God's sadness and suffering in this story.

In the Reading, we heard this lament of God: "O that you had listened to my commandments! Then your peace would have been like a river" (Is 48:18).

The same message returns in Psalm 81, which may have been composed in the same period: "O that my people would listen to me, that Israel would walk in my ways!... I would feed you with the finest of the wheat, and with honey from the rock I would satisfy you" (Ps 81:13, 16).

And the same message returns also on the Lord's lips: "Would that even today you knew the things that make for peace!" (Lk 19:42). Probably many of you are acquainted with the chapel in Jerusalem called *Dominus flevit*—the

Lord wept—on the Mount of Olives, which was built at the point where Jesus, seeing his city, reportedly spoke these words weeping. And history proves the truth of the divine lament.

The text of the Reading, like that of the Psalm, probably belongs to the time of the Exile. In his day, Jeremiah had clearly told the king and all the leading men of Israel: "Do not wage this war against Babylon, do not behave as though Israel were one of the major powers that can enter into war against Babel; do not do that, and do not think of it. Choose, instead, to stand totally with God. Keep the peace and remain in this country."

But they did not hear him; Israel did not listen to him, and it went into exile for seventy years and almost disappeared from history.

The Lord adopted as his own the same preaching of Jeremiah: "Do not start a conflict against the Romans; do not think that the Lord is a warrior who will give you military forces that you do not have. Take the path of repentance, faith, love, the path of communion with God; it alone can transform the world." But once again they did not listen, acting like Jeremiah's generation. They believed in Barabbas, and ultimately there was the destruction of Jerusalem; and Saint Luke says in the Gospel: "Jerusalem will be trodden down by the Gentiles, until the times of the Gentiles are fulfilled" (Lk 21:24).

These words are true even in our present day, in the age in which we live: "Why did you not listen?" The Lord could say that to us again. You could have avoided the disaster of the Communist regime that destroyed souls and your territory; you could have avoided that great disaster of National Socialism which is shameful for us, a wound for all humanity, above all of the conscience, particularly of the German people.

They did not listen, Lord. So we see how this divine lament is true, that at the same time it is not only a description of the past but a warning and a strong admonition to us and to our generation: "Listen, finally! All is not yet lost, listen and follow the Lord, the Lord of peace and not the lord of war."

This is a message that the Lord is saying especially to you, the new generation that has in its hands the keys to the future. It is a loud shout: "Listen, it is not true that there is an unchangeable destiny." It is human freedom to say Yes to changes for the better. And our duty is truly to listen, dear brothers and sisters, and to set out on this path courageously, to shout this to the world, even if it does not want to hear it; a least to make this lament and this appeal of the Lord heard, with all the weight of a past that we know sufficiently well.

Thus the messages of the Old and of the New Testament are the same; they say the same thing to different generations, and to us, too, it seems that this history is still open-ended in our hands. This is the great challenge that emerges from the texts of today's liturgy.

At the end of the Gospel, after the sadness of the men of so many generations and the danger that those of this generation, too, might say no, nevertheless, a message of joy appears: a promise of victory. The Lord says that, despite everything, "Wisdom is justified [i.e., proven to be just] by her deeds" (Mt 11:19).

In hearing this, we wonder first: Is it true that God is wise? Can we say that God is wisdom, that Christ, who endured the Cross, is wisdom? In reality, the Lord left the seeds of new life for his people and for the world, a leaven that would transform everything. And thus he founded a new form of living the faith.

The earthly Jerusalem was destroyed, yes, but from the Cross of Christ grows a new Jerusalem, a new city that is spread throughout the world, in small and also in great communities of believers. Animated by faith, a new city is growing, an image of the future Jerusalem.

"Wisdom is justified by her deeds." The first Christian communities are born; a new human spirit, love for the suffering and the poor that did not exist in the world before, a light of truth that illumines the paths of humanity, transforms the world, and, despite everything, conquers evil.

We have already spoken about the path of the lighted lamps, a path of light that spreads more and more in history. In this way, a new civilization, a new life was created. In the Book of Revelation it is written: "I looked, and behold, a great multitude ... clothed in white robes" (Rev 7:9). These are the ones "who have come out of the great tribulation" (Rev 7:14) and represent the new humanity. Wisdom was justified. God is wise; despite these defeats, the new humanity grows, and there is an increase in the gift of love, faith, and hope that Christ has given us.

Saint Luke, in his Gospel, records this message with a variation, saying: "Wisdom is justified by all her children" (Lk 7:35), the children of Christ, his brethren.

Beginning with the first martyrs, down to today's great witnesses to the faith, they all acknowledged Christ, the true Divine Wisdom. Thus this text invites us to be children of wisdom and to perform works of wisdom so as to transform the world.

Finally, the texts find a very concrete confirmation in the liturgy; the text of Psalm 81 says: "O that my people would listen to me.... I would feed you with the finest of the wheat, and with honey from the rock I would satisfy you." The Lord feeds us with the finest wheat, with himself, gives us this bread, gives himself in this little bit of wheat. He places himself into our hands, into our hearts.

Let us pray to the Lord that he may enlighten us, that he may permit us to listen to him and to carry out his Word. And thus to be his children, to perform his works, works of divine wisdom. Amen.

# MARY'S YES:
## "BLESSED IS SHE WHO BELIEVED"

*Lk 1:39–45*

With this Fourth Sunday of Advent, we have arrived at the summit of our journey toward the Feast of the Nativity of our Lord. Until now, we were guided by Saint John the Baptist, the Precursor, the great preacher of repentance and conversion, the last and greatest of the prophets, whose finger points out the long-desired Savior to the eyes of his disciples. Every year the holy Forerunner invites us once again to conversion, guides us toward the Lord, who always stands among us, while again and again we do not know him (cf. Jn 1:26).

Saint John is the great preacher of Advent, but, in the end, the Church entrusts us to the maternal guidance of the Mother of God. In Mary, the Old Testament becomes New, hope is transformed into fulfillment, having arrived in reality. She is the advent, the coming in person, that is, the living temple in which God dwells corporeally. Mary's Yes is the moment in which the Old Testament becomes New: this Yes is the gate through which God enters into the world. Our life is often far from the Savior; it moves "in darkness and in the shadow of death" (Lk 1:79); with our life we have not yet really arrived in the New Testament, in the presence of the Savior; even in the time of the New Testament, our life often remains in the Old. On the threshold of the Nativity, the Church invites us to see Mary, to learn from the Virgin Mother the passage from the Old to the New Testament.

What does Mary teach us for the journey of our life? To me it seems that the main point for us comes to light in today's Gospel, in the final words of Elizabeth: "Blessed is she who believed" (Lk 1:45). Mary believed unreservedly the word of God transmitted by the Archangel Gabriel. Here we find the essential difference between Eve and Mary. The dialogue between Mary and the angel contrasts radically with the dialogue between Eve and the serpent; we often find ourselves at the fork in the road between the two dialogues, between the two fundamentally opposed decisions that define the historical struggle between good and evil. Keeping in mind this background of history, we immediately see that Mary's faith is much more than a purely intellectual act. This faith is a personal decision that involves all the dimensions of human existence. Yes, Mary accepts with her intellect the supernatural truths communicated by the angel: the mystery of the Trinity, the mystery of the Incarnation, the mystery of her own Divine Motherhood. But the Virgin of Nazareth was able to accept these truths only because her life was in close harmony with God, united with God in a boundless trust, in a confidence born of love: "You are full of grace" means: your life is inundated by love, by charity, and charity is the Holy Spirit, the bond between Father and Son, the bond between God and his creature.

Mary is able to believe because she loves. Eve, in contrast, loses her faith in God's word and comes to experience the contrary at the moment when she opens her heart to the suspicion that God might not be entirely good. Poisoned by this suspicion, she seeks her happiness by setting herself against God; she fears God as a competitor who hinders her freedom, and she flees the presence of God. The path of sin, of unbelief, is always like this: our trust in God, our love for him diminishes, and the suspicion creeps in that perhaps through total obedience to the faith, to the Commandments, we are missing some of the beauty of the world and of life; God's presence becomes a threat, instead of a joy, and one flees this presence in order to construct one's own happiness. "Blessed is she who believed." Become like children, the Lord tells us, and thus he speaks about Marian faith, about this total Yes given to God without suspicion, without reserve, in a joyous and undivided confidence.

In reading Scripture, we can identify also two other important aspects of the act of faith. The dialogue between the angel and the Virgin concludes not only with a profession of faith but with an act of submission: "I am the handmaid of the Lord; let it be to me according to your word" (Lk 1:38). The word of God is not just information, the communication of truth; this word is a mission; it is a mandate. Faith has a practical consequence: it transforms life down to its foundation. God needs Mary, her Yes, her obedience. Faith is complete only when it becomes concrete obedience to the divine mandate. God awaits our Yes, awaits a faith that becomes life in the transformation of our will to the point of full conformity with his will.

Today's Gospel also adds: "Mary arose and went with haste into the hill country, to a city of Judah" (Lk 1:39). Faith tends to be communicated. Faith is dynamic, it sets us in motion toward others. The truth is not private property, an individual way of living. Truth is like the happiness destined for all, and therefore faith by its very nature is missionary. Certainly, the charisms are different: not all are apostles, not all are prophets, not all are preachers and teachers (compare 1 Cor 12:29). Yet no one believes alone, by himself. Each one must testify with his life through faith, and the humble, persevering faith of the contemplative communities is a beacon whose light speaks forcefully, even when the word does not arrive. In a time full of suspicions against God, against the Church, against the message of faith, a life based on trust without reserve and without suspicion becomes the strongest language in favor of faith; it becomes the door through which even today God enters into the world. Mary's Yes was born from a life of prayer, from a life lived in God's sight.

The sign of Mary, even today, opens the gates to the Savior. Let us follow her, and let us pray with the Church that "as the feast day of our salvation draws ever nearer, so we may press forward all the more eagerly to the worthy celebration of the mystery of your Son's Nativity" (from the Prayer after Communion).

# PLUNGING INTO GOD'S LOVE

*Heb 1:1–6; Jn 1:1–18*

Among the most ancient customs of the Christian liturgy is a little gesture at the beginning of the Preparation of the Gifts: a little drop of water is poured into the chalice with the wine. Originally this goes back simply to the Mediterranean peoples' ancient custom of never drinking wine without mixing it with water. Thus this drop of water connects us with the origin of the Eucharist: we do what Jesus Christ did. Even through such a little sign, it becomes evident that the Eucharist is not our invention and not something that we control; rather, it is acting with and being with Jesus Christ, who gave it to us. With the water, it is as though we returned to the Upper Room to do what the Lord did.

Over the course of history, there have been more and more reflections on this little gesture. From the eleventh century on, for example, preachers started to see it as an image of the mystery of the Nativity, the Christmas preparation, so to speak, of the Cross and Resurrection that become present among us in the Eucharist. Mixing water with wine seemed to be an interpretation of the great mystery of which Christmas speaks: God and man becoming one; the mystery of Christ, in whom a marvelous exchange occurs: God assumes human nature so that man can take part in the divine nature. The poor little drop of water, which sinks into the delicious, strong wine, appears to represent God's becoming man. Man, that poor being, is taken up into the ocean of the Divinity. Man stands in God's heart.

At every Mass, therefore, celebrants started to accompany this act of mixing water and wine with a Christmas prayer by Leo the Great, who in the early Church was the great theologian of the Feast of the Nativity. Thus Bethlehem, the hour of the Incarnation as the beginning of the mystery of Christ, was placed at the beginning of the real action of the Mass. And so it happens to this day; the liturgical reform has even deepened this relation. Indeed, in the Mass on Christmas Day, we have started reciting again the prayer of Leo the Great. Thus the gesture of mixing water and wine is connected even more clearly than in the past with the theme of Christmas Day.

If we look a little more closely at this prayer, we can bring something of the splendor of Christmas into everyday life and at the same time can come to understand better the deepest reason for the joy that we feel on Christmas. The prayer reads: "O God, who wonderfully created the dignity of human nature and still more wonderfully restored it, grant, we pray, that we may share in the divinity of Christ, who humbled himself to share in our humanity."

What do we learn here about Christmas? First of all this: that Christmas is at the same time and in the first place a feast of joy in creation, of thanksgiving for creation. God "wonderfully created" man. He can be redeemed at all only because this is so. He can assume in himself the whole universe and the whole universe can carry him only because he was wonderfully created. God could not have become a child if there had been no capacity for what is divine in the child, in man. The message of man's redemption is not a condemnation of the world and of creation but, rather, the strongest affirmation of them.

Man is capable of redemption, is capable of God, is "wonderfully created". Anyone who views Christianity only as fear of sin, man's self-condemnation, mistakes it for its rival, gnosis. "The spirit that always says no" (J. W. von Goethe, *Faust* I, v. 1338) is not the Spirit of Jesus Christ. Creation is wonderful; in ourselves, in our neighbor, in all that is created, it deserves our Yes. The purpose of Christmas is to open our hearts to creation; only in this way are they opened to Christ. Let us seek to rediscover what is beautiful, hopeful, pure, and great in children! Today there are a disturbing number of children who are not happy with their lives because they feel that they are not wanted, that they are perceived as nuisances, that there is no room for their freedom, which contrasts with ours, in an era when all we want is what can be regulated, what totally obeys our desires. "Wonderfully created"; accepting this phrase means having respect for creation. It has been entrusted to us, not to plunder it as we please, but to preserve it. The Latin verb *colere*, from which our word "culture" comes, originally means the relation of man to the earth, to his ancestors, and to the divinity. Christianity had to make some distinctions here, but it remains true that without respect for the earth, without respect for creation, there is no genuine culture.

What God wonderfully created, he "more wonderfully restored". How does it take place, this renewal of man for which everyone clamors today, however different the various expectations may be otherwise? Pope Leo the Great highlighted above all the magnificent character of this renewal. The Reading and the Gospel point in the same direction. God, who in creation already took the bold step of placing something outside of himself, of forming creatures who themselves are endowed with spirit and freedom, now takes a further, even greater step: he overcomes the gulf that separates Creator and creature. He himself becomes a creature. And the creature becomes God. Man's original dream *can* come true: to step out of himself, to leave all barriers behind, to be on familiar terms with God, to plunge into the sea of divinity. We must once again reflect on this greatness, indeed, on the absolutely thrilling aspects of the Christmas event. Christianity is not a men's club; it is not entertainment for one's free time, a charitable association, or an alternative political program. It is something more. God has called us. God wants us. If we leave that out, our Christianity becomes too modest and humanity becomes too little. All present-day desperation, in the final analysis, is based on the fact that we have lost the habit of even thinking about God, much less of considering him as a reality. But what remains is much too little. The only possible response is rebellion, the shout at what is Totally Other, even though it is addressed again and again to the void. Raising our sights to God, which to contemporary man seems such a useless thing, must not be eliminated from Christmas, must not be eliminated from our lives.

"Wonderfully restored"; this renewal is wonderful for us in another way, also, because it is completely different from our ideas of renewal. God did not create infallibly efficient structures. God did not create a utopian world that takes away from us in advance the burden of being human. He has spoken to us, he loves us. He hands himself over to us by becoming a child. What does this mean? God appeals to our humility, to our simplicity, to our love. Today's Reading says about this very same child that he is the reflection of the glory of God and the image of his nature. He "uphold[s] the universe by his word of power" (Heb 1:3). Without this return to simplicity, humility, trust, goodness, faith, there is no access to God. If we want to become like him, if we want redemption, we must take that child as our standard. It is no accident that the shepherds were the first ones to arrive at the manger, then, only afterward and much later, the Magi, and not at all the king, the merely learned, and the merely "wise". Without an ultimate willingness to be simple, to say Yes, to bow down and love, there is no redemption. Consequently, we should have great respect for all the simple and the poor of this world. They are closer to God than the powerful and the knowledgeable.

And so one final thing becomes clear. Throughout the liturgy of Christmas, the word "all" recurs. "All the ends of the earth have seen the victory [or salvation] of our God" (Ps 98:3). The Fathers of the Church gave a very profound interpretation of it. They say: God became man; therefore, only if we enter into what is common to all who have human nature do we find where the divine and the human touch. This means that I can have Christ only if I desire to have communion with all people. I cannot have him in opposition to the others. I can encounter him only if I do not shut myself up in myself but, rather, move toward the common foundation. I can have him only if I become authentically human. And I can be authentically human only if I accept what is common to all people. For this reason, the Church is part of the faith and not an external addition to it. For this reason, the mystery of Christ is "catholic" in the deepest sense, in other words, is an all-encompassing mystery. For this reason, part of being Christian is the very practical acceptance of the other, the rejection of all racial pride and of all class hatred. For this reason, the collect starting *Adveniat* is not just pasted onto the Feast of Christmas, perhaps to take advantage of an especially emotional atmosphere; rather, something like this is required by the very nature of the Christmas feast:

going to meet others, not only with words or sentiments, but with our actions. And for this reason, I cordially ask you in this hour to give this real sign of our fraternity, of our Yes to Christ: "All the ends of the earth have seen the [salvation] of our God" (Ps 98:3).

Let us return also for a moment to the drop of water in the Eucharistic wine! It represents the fact that man and God become one in Christ. It is, however, also a very practical direction for this day: let us very simply sink into the abyss of God, let us plunge into the wine of his love! This is what Christmas ought to be: relaxed freedom that allows itself to fall into this message, that allows itself to be permeated by the grace of this feast, and thus finds the "grace" and the "truth" (Jn 1:14, 17) that give us "life" (Jn 1:4).

# LENT AND THE EASTER SEASON

# THE CELEBRATION OF LENT

*Mt 6:16–18*

Every year Ash Wednesday is meant as a radio call sign in
our distraction, in our forgetfulness of what matters. It is
meant to jolt us awake to what we have neglected, to the
essential thing, to the Living God. "When a trumpet is
blown, hear!" says one of the passages from the prophets
that the Church reads in the season of Lent (Is 18:3). Ash
Wednesday is meant to be such a blast of God's trumpet,
so that we, as Saint Benedict of Nursia says, will listen with
trepidation to the voice of God that admonishes us every
day: "O that today you would listen to his voice! Harden
not your hearts" (Ps 95:7–8). Let us, therefore, open the
eyes and ears of our hearts to this exhortation of the Lord,
to this trumpet blast of his voice, applying it to ourselves in
our reflections, so that these words might touch our hearts
and show us the way during this season of Lent.

If we try to translate the Latin word *Quadragesima* and
render its meaning, we find ourselves in some difficulty.
The ancient expression "time of fasting" was no doubt
inadequate. The newer one, "Paschal season of penance",
is better, yet it does not say enough. Based on the semantic
field with which the liturgy interprets this term *Quadragesima*, we should perhaps translate it as "The Celebration of
the Forty Days". Actually, this semantic field is made up
mainly of three concepts: *sollemnia, celebrare,* and *sacramen-
tum*. By the term "sacrament", the language of tradition

means an event in the history of God with man, which in the Church has become a form of life wherein this event becomes reality and is made present again and again. By entering into this form of life, we touch the event and, thus, touch that point in history where the wall of transience is burst open, where the hand of God enters into this time.

*Quadragesima* is the "Celebration of the Forty Days"; it is entering into the sacrament of this time, into this extraordinary event in the history of God with man to which the number "forty" allusively refers.

So it becomes evident that *Quadragesima* represents and signifies something completely different from individual mortification or springtime dieting, even though it certainly can include this also. But the decisive point in these two things that I mentioned—individual mortification and a spring diet—is that here the focus is only on man himself, on his own ego. It is merely about self-actualization: with individual mortification, he wants to demonstrate mind over matter, his willpower. With dieting in the spring, he tries to take steps to improve his health, his outward success, and perhaps his physical appearance. But in this way, man can become neither completely just nor completely healthy, because the point of departure is wrong: the ego is at the center along with man's attempt to make himself. *Quadragesima* means correcting precisely this fundamental error under which the world labors, under which we all labor; it means to begin living less individually inasmuch as we surrender to the common "Celebration of the Forty Days", to the common form of Church life.

In this form of life, we touch the event of the years spent in the desert by the people of Israel, the mystery of the first love between God and his people. In it we touch the victory of Jesus Christ in the desert over the powers

that destroy the world. This is why *Quadragesima* is a celebration. Because of this, the Church follows the precept of
Christ: "When you fast, do not look dismal, . . . [but] anoint
your head" (Mt 6:16–17). She is guided by the words of
Saint Benedict: "With great spiritual joy we look forward
to the Holy Pasch" (*Rule*, 49, 7). In these forty days, we
celebrate the overcoming of the dualism between transcendence and immanence; the contact between God and the
world; the majesty of God, who is not the prisoner of his
eternity and is not the prisoner of the laws of the world
that he created, but who, through the heart of man, can
continually work in this world. We celebrate the freedom
of man, our freedom from the primordial law of selfishness,
freedom from the powers of death and, ultimately, from
the power of death that domineers by isolating the ego, by
isolating the parts of being. Finally we celebrate the victory
over the dualism between matter and spirit. To take part in
*Quadragesima* means that matter is made docile to the spirit
and that the spirit, by accepting, ratifying, and penetrating
matter, reaches a new greatness and depth, and one merges
with the other in a new creation, just as God willed.

*Quadragesima* is a celebration. This does not mean that
we flee from the sufferings of this world into an artificial
abstraction; on the contrary. Our celebration requires us to
accept the hunger and the needs of this world, by which
we seek to overcome the forgetfulness caused by living
comfortably and to wake up to the needs of the world.

But we do this by keeping our eyes fixed on the victory
of Jesus Christ and on the love of God, for the suffering of
the world can be overcome and is overcome only in his
Yes. Being anchored to heaven is as important as being
anchored to earth; let us not abandon love, which can
make even fasting a celebration, but we must not abandon,
either, the renunciation through which we go down and

touch the suffering of the world and of our time and the difficulties that are part of being human. This means entering into the victory of Jesus Christ in the desert: remaining stretched out, as he did, between the ends of the earth, drawing God's love down into the needs of the world, but also lifting up the needs of the world to the face of his mercy, which he has shown us in Jesus Christ.

"O that today you would listen to his voice! Harden not your hearts" (Ps 95:7–8). Accept the invitation to the celebration of the fast in which we prepare for our resurrection and the Feast of Eternal Life.

# "BEHOLD YOUR MOTHER!"
# THESE WORDS ARE ADDRESSED
# TO US, TOO

*Jn 19:25–27*

The Friday that precedes Good Friday is traditionally dedicated to the commemoration of Our Lady of Sorrows. The Mother guides us into the Paschal mysteries. Her part in these mysteries is compassion, and it is ours, too. If the Passion of our Lord is the fount of our salvation, then compassion is the chief way of drinking from this fount. From another perspective, the Passion of our Lord is God's compassion for us; compassion, therefore, becomes the gate that opens to us the heart of God.

Commemorating the Mother of God is not some form of sentimentalism that is foreign to the spirit of the great liturgy of Holy Week. If man's insensibility to the Divine Love, "the inability to grieve", is the psychological hotbed of sin, then the mystery of the Mother is the true antidote to the sickness; the mystery of Our Lady of Sorrows is part of the Paschal Mystery and of the Paschal liturgy. "Standing by the cross of Jesus were his mother, and his mother's sister, Mary the wife of Clopas, and Mary Magdalene" (Jn 19:25). We cannot be at the foot of the Cross, close by the mysteries of our salvation, without also being with Mary. There, Mary became the Mother of the Church. The Church was born when Jesus saw "his mother, and the disciple whom he loved standing near" (Jn 19:26).

The Prelature of the Holy Cross and Opus Dei invites its members to stand beside Mary at the Cross, so that the Lord might see us, so that we, too, might become disciples loved by Jesus, so that it may be said to us, also: "Behold your Mother!" (Jn 19:27a). It is no accident that the Evangelist writes: "After this Jesus, knowing that all was now finished" (Jn 19:28). All was finished from the moment when the disciple took Mary "to his own home". This passage of the Gospel not only prepares us for Good Friday; it also explains to us the heart of what it means for us to be Christians and is certainly particularly dear to the Prelature: It is the center of its mission, indicating the point where the work of God is accomplished.

Let us look more closely at what these words say to us: "the disciple whom he loved" (Jn 19:26). This text is like a signpost: Mary guides us to the Cross. The Eucharistic Presence of our Lord springs from the Cross. It is not possible to draw near to Christ while avoiding the Cross.

I am impressed with the words written by the Evangelist, that "standing by the cross of Jesus were" some women. The disciples flee, run away, while the women *stand*. They stand despite the mockery of their enemies; they stand despite the threats of the soldiers; they stand despite the sorrow, the darkness, despite all the questions in their hearts. To stand is an expression of courage, firmness, fidelity in love, even in the hour when all light is spent. Standing by the Cross: This is the first thing that we are told about Mary in this passage.

At the wedding feast of Cana (cf. Jn 2:1–11), Mary, with her fearless trust, patience, and humility, with her compassion and her intercession, had obtained from her Son the favor of anticipating his hour. His hour had not yet come, but in the superabundant gift of wine, Jesus anticipated the gift of his own hour, the gift of his blood that is the wine of life, the gift of blood in which he gives himself, his infinite love. In the Eucharist, the Lord, accepting the prayers of the Church, renews this miracle every time. The hour of his Reign has not yet come, but—anticipating the hour—he gives us his blood, himself, he who is the Kingdom of God in person, the *autobasileia*, as Origen says.

But let us return to ourselves. At Cana, our Lady obtained by her prayer the coming of the hour of Jesus in advance. Now, in this hour, beneath the Cross, she obtains, by her silent presence, pierced by the sword of compassion (see Lk 2:35), the fulfillment of all things, the new covenant. Here we see the power of prayer; we see the power of silence, of silent compassion. "When Jesus saw his mother..., he said...." The word of Jesus, his testament, is his response to seeing his Mother.

What does our Lord say? What is the meaning of his testament? Jesus identifies the disciple with himself. The disciple becomes the son, becomes what Jesus is. This marvelous identification is the fruit of crucified love. But this identification comes about in the entrusting of the disciple to Mary. Communion with Mary is the way to union with Jesus, the way of sacred exchange. In this entrusting of the disciple to the Mother from the height of the Cross, the Church is born, and she is always born in this way.

This entrusting has two aspects. On the one hand, the disciple of Jesus becomes also a disciple of his Mother. At the school of the Mother, he learns to be a son. From the Mother, he learns the words kept and pondered in her maternal heart (cf. Lk 2:19, 51). From the Mother, he learns not only the words, but also the significance of the *silence* of Jesus, the silence of thirty years in Nazareth, the silence of his eternal origin in the Father's bosom. From the Mother, who is the Church personified, he learns "to be Church". The school of the Mother is indispensable for becoming a son, for knowing the Father. On the other hand, Mary is entrusted to the disciple: "he took her to his own home", says the Evangelist. Saint Augustine notes at this point that the disciple, having left everything (cf. Mt 19:27), could not take the Mother in a material sense to "his house"—as the *Jerusalem Bible* translates it. Now what is "his" means "himself". He really takes her "with him", in his being, in his thinking and living, or, as the Holy Father says in his encyclical *Redemptoris Mater* (45): "He brings her into everything that makes up his inner life."

At the foot of the Cross, Mary once again becomes a mother; in the sorrow of her compassion, she begins a new maternity; the scriptural words come true: "Enlarge the place of your tent.... For you will spread abroad to the right and to the left, and your descendants will possess the nations" (Is 54:2–3). Mary's motherhood will last until the end of the world: Mary is not an abstract model of Holy Mother Church, just as the Church herself is not an abstraction. The Church is person in Mary and wishes to become person in us, too, entrusted by our Lord to Mary's maternal love. With regard to the disciple, our Lord says to Peter after the Resurrection: "If it is my will that he remain until I come, what is that to you?" (Jn 21:23). According to the Lord's will, the disciple remains, and with him the Mother remains.

In the Cross are fulfilled the words uttered by God at the beginning of human history: the words of blessing are fulfilled (cf. Gen 1:28), and the curse is overcome (cf. Gen 3:14–19). Jesus, born of woman, crushes the head of the serpent that strikes at the heel (Gen 3:15). The serpent's apparent victory, the death of the Redeemer, is actually his ultimate defeat: the head of the serpent, the arrogance of wanting to be like God, is crushed by the Son's humility and love. The curse disappears and is replaced by the new words: "Blessed are you among women, and blessed is the fruit of your womb!" (Lk 1:42). The ultimate place of blessing is the Cross. Today's liturgy, the liturgy of Lent, is the Church's invitation to all of us to stand by the Cross together with Mary. Let us also listen to these words: "Woman, behold your son!" Let us accept these words: that way we will be sons of the blessing, and the serpent will do us no harm (cf. Mk 16:18). Amen.

# JOSEPH'S FAITH

*Mt 1:16, 18–21, 24*

The saints are the permanent catechesis given to us by God over the course of history: the saints, in fact, are the ever-new translation of the Word of God into human life; in the saints, the Word becomes life, flesh and blood; in seeing the saints, we can understand the true intentions of the Word of God.

Saint Joseph was privileged to be very close to the Lord, and so the essential points of Christian life shine through in an exceptional way in his life, too. Saint Joseph lives the Christian life before the outward origin of Christianity; he bears within himself the hope, the faith, the patience of Abraham, of the patriarchs and prophets, and, thus, like Simeon and like Anna, stretches out toward the Lord. The faith of these simple, silent, and imperturbable believers opens the gate for Christ. The great wise men of those days and the powerful men in the political world did not know Jesus, or else they opposed the announcement of him; the simple believers held the key of the ages in their hands, and, in the crisis of a world full of conflicts and dangers, their faith opened up the path of salvation.

But let us look a little more closely at the figure of Saint Joseph. How is this faith of his manifested? What does a life guided by this faith look like? The Gospels do not say much about Saint Joseph, but in a few words we find a great wealth of insight. An initial observation: the Gospel says that Saint Joseph was a just man. Since he does not know the mystery of the Incarnation, he must, according to the Law of Moses, dismiss his betrothed who is pregnant. Since he is just not only externally but also in the depth of his heart, even though he follows the Law, he does not want to repudiate his bride. Humanly speaking, his respect, his affection for this woman remains. The justice of Saint Joseph is a humane justice. Therefore, he seeks an application of the Law that takes into account respect for the other and opens up for him a new path in life. Saint Joseph is just: an upright, sober, dependable man, a profoundly humane man. His justice is also goodness. For him, the Law is not an instrument with which to claim his own rights, his own benefit; in his life, the Law is the means employed by a sincere, upright, and generous goodness, without grand words.

But where does this justice come from? What is the source of this type of life? In the language of the Old Testament, the word "just" corresponds to the New Testament word "faithful". "Just" is the honorific title of the great believers, starting with the patriarchs Abraham, Isaac, and Jacob, down to the Messiah. The just man is one who accepts the Word of God and lives it, because in those days the Word of God was essentially the Law, God's legislation. Therefore, the name "just" for Saint Joseph means that Joseph was a true believer. God was a concrete reality in his life. His closeness to God, his intimate openness to the living God was the source of his uprightness with regard to others. Joseph was not one of those men described in the Psalms who say that God does not care: "There is no God.... God has forgotten, he has hidden his face, he will never see it" (Ps 10:4, 11). How familiar this mentality is today, a mentality in which one does not absolutely deny the existence of a supreme

being, but this existence is obscured because we are sure
that God has no time for us, that God is not concerned
about us, that God does not care. For this mentality, only
success matters; in a life without the hope of eternity,
one must take the greatest possible advantage of this life;
and justice goes to ruin.

Saint Joseph is just because he is a believer. It seems to
me that the words of the Letter to the Hebrews regard-
ing Noah could serve as a portrait of Saint Joseph: "By
faith Noah, being warned by God concerning events as
yet unseen, took heed and constructed an ark for the sav-
ing of his household" (Heb 11:7); and this Holy Family is
the true ark of salvation for the whole world, for all ages.
Building an ark of salvation. This is a program for us, too.
Every living parish is an ark of salvation; Christian families
are arks of salvation; and it is always by faith that an ark
is built, that we are warned about things that we do not
yet see.

With these words, we have arrived at the core of the
figure of Saint Joseph. The first response of the Gospel
to our inquiry into the physiognomy of this man was:
he was a just man. To the question, "Where did his justice come from?", we received the answer that he was a
believer, guided by the Word of God. The question still
remains: What is the path by which to become a believer?
If we meditate on the few words of the Gospel that speak
about Saint Joseph, we can say: this man was interiorly
vigilant with regard to the hidden presence of God, or—as
the Fathers of the Church say—the ears of his heart were
open. With this sensibility of an upright heart, he listened
to the Lord's promptings and was warned about things
unseen! Thus, he could disdain public opinion and fearlessly live according to God's justice. The believer is a truly
prudent man, since he is vigilant with regard to the most

important dimensions of reality, which, however, are hidden to a superficial mentality that is orientated only toward the present moment. Faith is also a sensitivity of the heart to the profundity of reality that is creation. In the noise of our time, we must learn anew this true prudence, this true realism, this true sensitivity.

The Church always celebrates the Feast of Saint Joseph during Lent, and it seems to me that Joseph is a Lenten saint in a very profound sense. Saint Joseph's faith is the faith of Noah, that is, faith within a world that is opposed to God, within a dark world where God seems to be absent. In the figures of the Emperor Augustus, King Herod, and King Archelaus, the powerful of the world enter into God's life and determine his journey, the course of his flight into exile. Joseph accepted a mission although he could not see the fulfillment of it, since he died before the public life of Jesus. He lived for the things that were not yet seen. Only with an open, vigilant heart that is sensitive to the hidden yet very real presence of the Lord can one remain faithful and just in a world that is so contrary to the faith. And *this* world is especially in need of just men. An Old Testament prayer comes to mind that no doubt was well known to Saint Joseph; a prayer that characterizes the spirituality of this saint. The man who prays here sees the fortune of those who say "God does not care", sees his own poverty, and hears the atheists' mockery. But being deeply rooted in his justice, he says to God: "May their belly be filled with what you have stored up for them; may their children have more than enough.... As for me, I shall behold your face in righteousness; when I awake, I shall be satisfied with beholding your form" (Ps 17:14–15).

There is no envy for other men's fortune when one has discovered the true good, the pearl of great price: "beholding your face". Let us pray to God that we, too, might find the pearl, that we, too, might become just, that we, too, might be able to pray: "I shall behold your face in righteousness; when I awake, I shall be satisfied with beholding your form."

# "DO WITH ME WHAT YOU WILL, ONLY GRANT THAT I MAY LOVE YOU COMPLETELY"

*Jn 13:1–15*

*Greeting [Statio]:*

In every celebration of the Eucharist, we proclaim the death of the Lord; in every Mass, we commemorate the night on which he was betrayed. But this evening we consider more than usual the human background of that night and the significance of the fact that he lets himself be delivered into the hands of men. Even today he delivers himself into the hands of men, into our hands. And since we can never be worthy to receive him adequately, let us begin by asking him to help us, to grant us his forgiveness.

*Homily:*

An Austrian priest friend of mine recently published a memoir about his mother, who in a difficult time, in needy circumstances that are hard for us to imagine today, brought into the world eleven children, of whom eight chose the way of priesthood and religious life of their own accord. The most striking thing in the book is the account of the mother's testament. On the last day of her life, in the morning, she participated as always in the celebration of the Eucharist and received the Body of the Lord; then she

turned to her usual everyday tasks. In the evening, as was
her custom, she blessed the photos of her children together
with her husband and then went into the kitchen to fix
herself a cup of coffee. After a while, she was found there
on the floor, unconscious, and three hours later she died.
But the upsetting thing is that on the table there was a card
that one of her children had written to her not long before;
in one corner that was left blank, in weak but still quite
legible script, she had written: "Do with me what you will,
only grant that I may love you completely."

Evidently she had sensed that she was about to be
overpowered by the destructive force of death, by unex-
pected physical collapse, and she had taken the last available moment to say one last word to her loved ones, so
as to define herself once again. And she had transformed
that moment, on the threshold of death, that moment
of extreme fear in which she was about to be overpowered by the unfathomable, into full freedom: "Do with
me what you will, only grant that I may love you completely." If someone knew nothing else about that woman's career, he could immediately tell from this what a
journey she had made in order to be able to find at the
conclusion—with all her characteristic simplicity—such
greatness, such maturity and freedom. Nor is there any
need for an explanation in order to realize how from a
life like this a sort of radioactivity of goodness must have
emanated that still sustains and moves an entire generation, making it, in turn, radioactive of goodness. Furthermore: even if we did not know it, we could intuit it; we
would have to presume that such freedom grew in her
by looking at Jesus Christ and by living in Jesus Christ.
Indeed, that was her journey. She had lived with the liturgy and had sought Christ on the basis of it. And since
freedom like that came from Christ, she thereby refers

back to him again, points him out, and helps us to see him better, to understand him more.

It seems to me that the message of today's Gospel—the message of the final hours of Jesus Christ on earth: "Having loved his own ..., he loved them to the end"—can be understood thanks to that sentence and the dynamic that it contains better than on the basis of learned commentaries. And thanks to it, we can understand better the mystery of the Mount of Olives, in which all the fear of a creature who finds himself alone confronting nothingness is turned into freedom. Into the freedom of a greater love: "Not my will, but yours, be done" (Lk 22:42). And since this love of his was not only an experience and a reflection of the Father's love, but was the creative love of the Son, therefore from it proceeds a radioactivity of goodness that reaches the very ends of the earth, that is indestructible, that forms the narrow but reliable island of redemption from which comes the light that helps us to live.

"Do with me what you will, only grant that I may love you completely." Based on this, we manage to understand the Lord: the original gesture of that love with which the slave at the door renders service to the guests who are expected, for whom—as the dust and the sweat of the Orient demand—he washes their feet so as to make them able of take part in the banquet. He waits for us to cleanse us of the dust and the sweat of our lives so as to make us capable of standing together, capable of taking a place at his table. There is something surprising in the account of the washing of the feet. It has often been repeated that it has all the characteristics of the institution of a sacrament. There is an outward sign, there is grace, there are the words: "Do as I have done." And thus at times some have considered the possibility of defining it as a sacrament. But, in reality, this is not an eighth sacrament that had been forgotten and discarded; rather, it manifests the sacrament that he himself is. The sacrament of his love demonstrated in the ordeal of his Passion and death, a sacrament that is given to us above all in the Eucharist, in which he gives himself as love; this sacrament of the Eucharist that, on the other hand, is closely connected to the sacraments of conversion— to Baptism and Penance. And thus, if we look at this account in which the mystery of the Eucharist is shown in its profundity, we can also understand in a renewed way what it means to receive the Eucharist. Moreover, the scene of Holy Thursday, the washing of the feet, year after year, in the liturgy of this day, in the final analysis has the meaning of opening our eyes once again, of teaching us to understand better what it means to celebrate the Eucharist. Celebrating the Eucharist means entering into love. And one cannot enter into love without having left oneself, without having left egotism behind. Entering into love always means also learning to say: "Do with me what you will." And thus, in order to make sure that we celebrate the Eucharist properly, we will always have to evaluate, above all, the extent to which we ourselves have been drawn into the radioactivity of love.

In his encyclical *Redemptor hominis*, the Holy Father demonstrated how Jesus summarized his whole message in two sentences: "Believe in the gospel" and "Be converted." This is the invitation to enter into the joy of his love, the invitation to enter into the Eucharist. But the Jesus who says to us "Come" and who offers himself to us is the same one who also says, "Be converted." Be liberated from yourselves so that the radioactivity of love can find room and strength in you. The Church's faith has a name for this new radioactivity; this name is the Holy Spirit. The Holy Spirit is the love that gushes from him, love in person. And in this encyclical the pope exhorts us

to enter into it as into the space of redemption: to transform the world on the basis of the Holy Spirit, by invok-
ing him and by living together with him. To oppose the
defilement and the poisoning of the world with this new,
transforming radioactivity that his salvation alone can be.
Because the world is not redeemed by a mental attitude
that is wholly concentrated on its own demands and claims
or by the resulting revolutions, but solely by God's "men
of violence", who are violent in their faith and love, as the
pope says, referring to the words of Jesus (see Mt 11:12).
In this encyclical, he has also made for us a diagnosis of our
time that is consistent with the specific character of this
evening. He says that our time is the time of a new Advent.
The word Advent calls to mind, first of all, the consolation
and the joy of expectation because of the Lord's approach.
Think of Mary's expectancy and of the silent, gentle light
that emanates from it. But Advent has another aspect, too.
It also means the night of the Mount of Olives. It also
means finding oneself alone at the threshold of nothingness
and death. It means a solitary struggle against the powers
of chaos in the hour in which wicked men are at work and
the disciples are asleep. Blaise Pascal, who suffered from
illness himself for many years and constantly experienced
the night of loneliness, the night of the Mount of Olives,
wrote: "Jesus is in agony until the end of time."[1] Even
today he is on the Mount of Olives. And in order to notice
this, it is enough to open our eyes a bit. How many persons today are thrust into loneliness because of their faith,
because of their conscience; how many are thrust into fear
of the nothingness and the destruction that threaten them.
And we must also say that his disciples are asleep because

---

[1] Blaise Pascal, *Pensées*, in *Oeuvres complètes*, ed. Jacques Chevalier, Bibliothèque
de la Pléiade (Paris: Gallimard, 1954), 1103–1348, here fragment 736, 1313.

they are unwilling or unable to acknowledge the Lord's loneliness, the danger and the threat to which his followers are exposed. In all of them, there is an Advent that calls for transformation, that calls for redemption through the merciful love of Jesus Christ.

So this evening, let us look at the Lord who remained alone for us. Let us look at those who are alone for him and with him.

Let us pray that he may abolish the fear that is still left in our souls, although we often try to stifle it with grand words, and that drives us to distance ourselves from him, to flee, because we are afraid of standing with him.

And that he may give us true, redemptive freedom, the kind that is capable of saying now with him: "Do with me what you will. Only grant that I may love you completely."

# WHEN GOD KNEELS DOWN
# BEFORE US

*Jn 13:1–15*

The message of the washing of the feet does not start only with the Cenacle. It runs through the entire life of Jesus. It is clearly evident the first time, in the life of Jesus, during a banquet in which he observes how disrespectfully and tactlessly the invited guests elbow each other so as to take the places of honor (Lk 14:7–11). The Lord tells his disciples that they must not act that way. They must calmly go to take the lowest places, letting the host be the one to ask them to come higher. When he says this, he is suggesting something quite different from a slightly inhibited modesty. Certainly, there is also a rather sarcastic lesson in manners, given the lack of tact that he finds. Basically tact, courtesy, is a sign of humanity, sometimes its last bastion.

But it becomes clear that there is much more to it when Luke says that this teaching of Jesus was a parable (Lk 14:7). In this struggle for the places of honor, the Lord sees an image of world history, in which men struggle for power and wealth, in which everyone wants to be on top, wants to do violence and to elbow others out of the way in order to take possession, because they think that in this way they will become free like God, so to speak. In reality, they ruin themselves and the world because they pillage the earth while being crushed in a spiral of violence.

When Jesus came into the world, he did not do that. He chose the lowest place. He was born in a stable. He lived as a laborer among the poor of Israel. He taught among publicans, sinners, the despised. He surrounded himself with fishermen. And he died outside the gates of the city between two criminals. This is where the true image of God is manifested. Because the true God is not a tyrant who does violence whenever he likes, who stands there self-absorbed in order to assert himself. The true God is self-giving, Trinitarian love. Paul Claudel has expressed this splendidly: the lance of Longinus, he says, went beyond the Cross. It opened the heart of God, and it penetrated to the very heart of the Trinity.

We find again at the Lord's Supper the same act of seeking the places of honor that we observed at the Pharisee's dinner. The Evangelists tell us that the disciples argued about the first place (Lk 22:24–30). They represent in miniature, so to speak, once again among themselves, the tragedy of world history. With this the Gospel means to tell us that the world exists even in the Church. We should not be surprised if the image of world history extends into the Church, too, and can make its way to what is holiest, to the Eucharist. The Lord contrasts this, however, with the transformation of values that he himself is. He has already decided on his place even at the Last Supper. His place is not the place of the gentleman, the place of the powerful, the place closest to the full serving dish, or the most comfortable one. He does not even take a place at table, but goes around the room like a servant who gives out the food, who gives out himself.

This is what the account of the washing of the feet in Saint John's Gospel means. The Lord washes away from the feet of his disciples the sweat and the filth of everyday life, so as to make them ready for the banquet. Even more than the other Evangelists, John shows that this is not just an isolated moral act. The Lord himself throughout his whole life is the act of washing our feet. His essence is bending down to us; his being is humility. Indeed, the fact that he, the Son of God, is here as a man is based on the fact that he has taken off the cloak of his glory, that he has girded himself with the coarse linen of human nature. And now he kneels down in front of us, his creatures. With his own body he washed us in his suffering, he cleansed us from the stench of our pride and from the filth of our egotism, thus preparing us for the feast of God's love.

"For I have given you an example, that you also should do as I have done to you" (Jn 13:15). This sentence is more than a moral exhortation to perform moral acts. It is the very foundation of being Christians, an introduction into communion with Jesus Christ. It is the humility of bending down. We can identify with him only if we enter into this dynamism, only if we ourselves become humble. Without humility, it is not possible to believe. To say Yes to the Mystery in the midst of a world that does not acknowledge it, to say Yes to the limits of our reason, to the unfathomableness of a God who kneels down before us, is not possible without humility. And just as there is no faith without humility, so too there is no love. Everyone knows this: part of love is knowing how to put up with something, knowing how to remain silent, knowing how to accept humiliation. Love can exist only in great humility. And since without faith and love man has nothing to hope for, and since nevertheless neither one can exist where there is no humility, therefore humility is also the prerequisite for our hope. In this way the Gospel of Holy Thursday links humility to the very essence of Christianity. It is the true soil without which it is not possible to be Christian.

Today, though, we hardly dare to say that. Together with chastity and obedience, humility is par excellence the most heretical and forbidden word bar none. It is targeted by the mockery of Nietzsche, who depicts Christians, with their humility, as deformed, inhibited people who do not dare to stand up and have neither courage nor greatness. To the Christian ideal, Nietzsche opposes the ideal of the superman who has backbone and stands upright. It is also targeted by the critique of Karl Marx, who sees humility as a tool by which man exploits man, a means for keeping power, a means of preventing everyone from knowing and demanding his own rights.

Now, of course, humility is misunderstood if by that one means the inhibited, false modesty that thinks it is incapable of anything great, that does not dare to acknowledge the greatness that we have and that therefore sinks into the faintheartedness of envy and insincerity. But this is not what the Lord meant.

The Christian meaning of humility was aptly defined by Saint Benedict in his *Rule* when he says: humility means overcoming forgetfulness. Humility means opposing the forgetfulness that would like to make us forget that we are creatures who can live only from his gift and who can exist and keep the world tolerable only by serving. Someone who thinks of man only as an autonomous being, a law unto himself, is dreaming and eluding reality. The law of the Son says: "Not my will, but yours, be done" (Lk 22:42). Someone who tries to bring man to an emancipation in which he thinks that he owes nothing to anyone and bases everything on his own law and on his own will, is dreaming and eluding reality, animated by a false pride.

The first truth about man is that he is created. He cannot create by himself the best of himself but only receive it. He lives by reciprocal giving and by reciprocal grace.

Because this is the case, another part of humility is the courage to acknowledge gratefully our own goodness and our own greatness, knowing that this very thing is not our doing, but that we received it as a gift. One who is able to acknowledge this is also able to acknowledge without envy the goodness in others, because he also knows that it is a gift from the same hand, a gift for all, a gift of God who wants to make us great and rich. Another part of humility is the courage to stand up for truth, the courage not to bow to the appearances of opinion, not to take the image as one's criterion, but to remain faithful to the truth. The Gospel of Saint John tells us that the real motive for the rejection of Jesus was the fear of "doxa ton anthropon" (Jn 12:43), the fear of human opinion, which means the dominion of appearances.

Appearances dominate in our time, too. Has it not become usual in politics for what matters to be, not the impact on reality, but the impact on the *media*? And, consequently, that action is taken, not for reality, but for the sake of appearances and public opinion? Is there not already some danger that we will submit to this dictatorship of appearances? That we no longer dare to detach ourselves from these appearances and from the images that they demand, thus becoming slaves of an increasing lack of truth? Pride does not make people free, but gives opinion power over reality. It puts dominion into the hands of the dictatorship of appearances, making us its slaves.

On the other hand, humility means not to seek out or follow current opinion, not to be frightened by the last place, but to take God, the truth, as the principal criterion of judgment. Humility means remaining steadfast, based on this courage: suffering and thereby becoming free in it. Holy Thursday entrusts to us this commandment for our everyday lives. Let us dare to learn humility again! The humility that, in the confession of our sins, allows the Lord to wash our feet; the humility that gratefully acknowledges God's gifts in us and in others; the humility that does not bow to appearances and does not live by opinions; the humility that makes us free through the Lord. Only where there is humility does one breathe, because only a humble man gives himself, because only he is able to believe, and because only he is able to love; because he finds the courage to serve even when there is no recompense in return and no legal obligation to do so.

About thirty years ago, the great scholar Heinrich Schlier, in his autobiographical account of his conversion, wrote that one of the signs that led him on the way to the Catholic Church was the fact that a Catholic, let us say, is humble and devout: "Even the men kneel down", he wrote. Would we still find this sign among us today? One of the most beautiful formulations of what Christ's humility means as our hope is found in one of our German *Passionslieder* (hymns sung in Passiontide): "What wondrous punishment is this to render! For erring sheep is slain the Shepherd tender; the Lord, the just one, for the servant payeth, who Him betray."[1] We live because of this humility, let us live for it!

---

[1] J. S. Bach, *St. Matthew Passion*, chorale no. 46.

# "I HAVE RISEN,
# AND NOW I AM ALWAYS WITH YOU"

*Ps 118; Mk 16:1–7*

"This is the day which the LORD has made; let us rejoice and be glad in it" (Ps 118:24). These luminous Paschal words with which the Church today gladly responds to the announcement of the Resurrection are taken from an Old Testament liturgy of thanksgiving celebrated at the gate of the Temple and preserved for us in a psalm that is completely illuminated by the Mystery of Christ. It is the Psalm from which the *Benedictus* and the *Hosanna* are taken, too; it is also the psalm of the "stone which the builders rejected" that "has become the cornerstone" (Ps 118:22). What is special about this psalm, however, lies in the fact that the rescue of an unknown individual, who from death has risen again to life, opens anew the gates of salvation for the people; in this way, the rescue of the individual becomes a liturgy of thanksgiving, a new beginning, a new gathering of the people of God for the benefit of them all. Within the Old Testament, there is no answer to the question about who this personage is. Only in terms of the Lord, in terms of Jesus Christ, does the entire psalm acquire its logic, its clear meaning. He is the one who in fact descended into the night of death, who was surrounded and battered by all the tribulation of sin and death. He is the one who, by rising again, threw open the gates of salvation and now invites us to pass through the gates of salvation and to give thanks together with him. He himself personally is the new day that God created for us; by means of him, God's day shines into the night of this world. Easter day and every Sunday make this day present, are an encounter with the living, Risen Lord, who as God's day comes into our midst and gathers us.

But let us see now how the Evangelist, whose Good News we have just heard, describes the dawning and the beginning of this new day (Mk 16:1–7). Here are the women who go to the tomb, the only ones who, well beyond death, have the audacity to be faithful: simple and humble souls who have no good name to defend, no career to which to aspire, no possessions to safeguard; and who therefore have the courage of love to go once again to someone who was disgraced and now has been lost in order to offer him the final service of love. In the haste of the Day of Preparation, as the feast day drew near, they had been able to do only the first and most necessary tasks of the burial, but they had not been able to finish the rituals, which they intend to complete only now: the funeral laments, which could not be intoned during the feast but now, as an accompaniment of love, lead them into the unknown and must protect them as a force for good; and then the anointing, which is like a useless gesture of love meant to give immortality (indeed, the anointing aims to preserve from death, to preserve from decay, as though they were trying to keep the dead man alive with all the helplessness of love and, nevertheless, could not). The women have come, therefore, to show him once again their lasting love and, nevertheless, to bid him farewell while commending him to the earth from which he would no longer return, to the night of death from which no one comes back.

But when they arrive, they discover that Someone Else, another stronger love has anointed him, that the words of the Psalm have come true for him: "You do not give your holy one to see corruption" (Ps 16[15]:10, see Douay-Rheims version). Since he himself stands in the circle of Trinitarian love, he was anointed with the eternal love and therefore could not remain in death. Indeed, this love alone is the power that is life and that gives life for eternity. And so for him are fulfilled, also, the other words of the psalm that the Church now uses as the entrance antiphon of the Mass on Easter day: *Resurrexi, et adhuc tecum sum....* "I have risen, I am still with you ... [you] lay your hand upon me.... You have searched me and known me (Ps 139:18b, 5, 1). In the Old Testament, this is the prayer of someone half-frightened and half-astonished, who, in his wrestling with God, realizes that there is nowhere he can flee from God's presence. If he traveled to the end of the sea and if he managed to descend into the netherworld thinking that he would finally be far from God, he would be all the more in God's sight, which embraces everything and from which it is impossible to flee anywhere.

But what had remained here half obscure, what was half fear and half joy, is now definitively fulfilled in the great grace of divine love, because Jesus was capable of the impossible: with his love he has traversed all the ends of the earth. He descended into the kingdom of the dead. And since he himself is the Son, the love of God descended with him and became present everywhere, for this reason, precisely in this descent, and as the one who descends, he is the one who arises, who has risen, and who can now say: "Resurrexi, et adhuc tecum sum" (I have risen and I am still with you, forever).

He now pronounces these words of the psalm in a two-fold sense. On the one hand, he addresses the Father: "I have risen, you are always with me, as I am always with you, and I brought human nature, the very being of man,

into eternal love, so that through me it is always with you."
But what he said to the Father he says at the same time to
us: "I have risen, and now I am always with you." He says
this to each one of us. There is no night in which I would
not be there. And there is no fear or any distance from
God in which I would not be there. Be consoled, I have
risen and am always and forever with you. I think that
we ought to take to heart these great words of the liturgy
that Christ drew from the predictions and the hope of the
Old Testament, transforming them into his Paschal words,
and to know that, whatever happens, he says to each of us
quite personally: "Yes, I have risen, and I am always with
you, wherever your paths bring you."

The women—we heard—had not been able to complete the rite of burial on the Day of Preparation, on the
eve of the feast day. Others, in contrast, wanted the matter
to be finished once and for all, wanted this Jesus to be sent
away forever and never to return: his enemies! And thus
Jews and Gentiles together had made sure that the stone
placed at the entrance to the tomb was well secured and
immovable and sealed. Christ had to be exiled forever to
the past by means of the impenetrable stone, so that he
could not return.

And the same thing continues to happen even today and
in every era. Marxism tried to set against Christ the stone
of so-called scientific materialism and to make it his tomb.
This stone of apparent science was supposed to bury forever
the life-giving spirit of the Risen Lord, so that he would be
relegated to the past and would not disturb the Babylonian
dream of self-creating humanity. But the liberalism and
the practical materialism of the Western world basically
do the same thing. With all sorts of pseudo-scientific
proof, with the laws of nature that cannot admit something like that at all, the argument goes, they too wanted

to affix the seal: they wanted no one to dislodge this stone; they wanted there to be no way around this stone, so that by dint of our knowledge, Christ would be definitively banished and confined to the past so that he could no longer "enlighten" us. But God's strength is mightier than all the stones in the world. The Spirit of God rolled away the stone of all these powers. Christ rose, and the stone became the door through which God enters into the world and through which we turn our gaze to him; it became the gate beside which we now can celebrate a true "liturgy of the gate", a liturgy of thanksgiving and joy. But the gate of the Resurrection is a reality present in the Eucharist; in it Christ's death and his Resurrection continue to be in this world and to open onto God. Because what happened once is valid forever. The wall of death and the powers of death are smashed. Christ enters, and in Holy Communion we can enter with him into his world, into the world of the eternal love that conquered death.

Again and again he shows us manifestly, too, that he is stronger than all the powers of this world. There was Marxism with all its frightening power, with its scientifically devised power to watch over individuals and to hinder any spiritual movement of their own; with all the strength of its powerful military arsenal, its divisions, its police, its economic power and worldwide politics, which was like a stone that no one could have removed. But Christ overturned it. God's divisions, in other words, the invisible company of those who love and suffer because of their own faith, was stronger than the military divisions with all the terrible armaments of this world. Yes, Christ showed us once again: "I have risen, and I am stronger than all the powers of this world! No stone, regardless of where it comes from and however forcibly it may be sealed, can resist me."

Finally, there is a third element: the women arrive at the tomb, find it empty, but do not encounter the Risen Lord himself; instead, there is a messenger, an angel of God who tells them: "He is not here; for he has risen" (Mt 28:6). This angel is the precursor of the Evangelists, of the apostles; he is the precursor of the priests and of the bishops of the Church; it continues to be their responsibility to stand opposite the overturned stone, to understand its significance, and to announce: he is risen; he is risen, and he is not here, in the world of the dead. He goes before you. And anyone who seeks him here, in the world of the dead, will not find him. Anyone who tried, so to speak, to take him in his hands, to analyze him and to understand him with documents, as some scientific methods of interpreting Scripture try to do, would exile him precisely to the world of the dead, would try to find him in what is dead, in what can be dissected, taken apart, and analyzed under the microscope: and of course they could not discover him there. Because the Lord is not dead but, as Paul says, is "a life-giving spirit" (1 Cor 15:45). He is the Risen Lord who has brought flesh into the power of the living God, of the Holy Spirit.

He is not a dead object, but the living movement of life, and we can encounter him only if we allow ourselves to be guided and moved by him. We can encounter him only if we follow him. "He is not here.... He is going before you to Galilee" (Mt 28:6–7). Only by following him do we see him. Only when we travel with him does he make himself visible and touchable to us.

Gregory of Nyssa once put it marvelously. He harks back to that mysterious Old Testament passage in which Moses says to God: "I wish to see you." And God replies: "You cannot see my face; for man shall not see me and live.... You shall see my back" (Ex 33:20, 23). Gregory of

Nyssa asks himself what this means and answers: "Someone who follows sees the back of the one whom he follows.... To follow God wherever he leads is to see God." To see God's back, therefore, simply means to follow Christ. We see the mystery of God by following Christ, by obeying him and, in obeying him, by walking behind him and therefore with him.[1]

But where? In the first place: he goes before us to Galilee. After the days of the feast in Jerusalem, he returns to his world; this means that we follow him by going into our world and giving witness to him there. We can preserve faith itself only by giving it to others. Only in giving do we receive it. Because only in that way do we follow him.

But there is another indication that Paul gives in his Letter to the Colossians, the epistle about Easter night: "Seek the things that are above, where Christ is, seated at the right hand of God" (Col 3:1). Following the Risen Lord means: ascending. Following Christ is not just any moral program. Following Christ means following him, the Risen Lord, into the communion of life of the Triune God. No man, of course, is capable of this by himself. Because we cannot get there by the power of our footsteps or of wings that we have made. But we can ascend by participating in the life of the living body of Christ, the Church, which, being his body, is always in this movement of ascent. We can ascend by allowing ourselves to be enveloped and carried by his body in the communion of the sacraments, in the communion of the Holy Eucharist. Following is above all else a communion of faith, life, and love with the living Church, with the presence of the Lord in the Most Blessed Sacrament.

[1] Gregory of Nyssa, *The Life of Moses*, PG 44:408D.

It follows, then, that we carry this movement into our everyday routine, and in it we are the ones who ascend; that we do not allow our gaze to be captivated by everyday things but transcend this horizontal dimension and venture into the vertical dimension of the new opening to the living God, to the Risen Lord; thus tearing open the world again and again so that the gate that he has opened might be visible, so that heaven might illumine the earth. And the earth will be livable and humane only by becoming more than human, only in becoming open to the divine, to the grace of the Risen Lord.

"This is the day which the LORD has made; let us rejoice and be glad in it." Today let us thank the Lord for the grace of his light, for the day of his Resurrection. And let us pray to him that the joy of the Resurrection, the light of this new day, might accompany us always, that we might learn to follow him and, thus, that we might see.

# ORDINARY TIME

# "BLESSED ARE YOU
WHEN MEN HATE YOU"

*Jer 17:5–8; 1 Cor 15:12, 16–20; Lk 6:17, 20–26*

In the third-to-last canto of *The Divine Comedy*,[1] Dante speaks about someone perhaps from Croatia who is so fascinated by the face of Christ imprinted on Veronica's veil that he can no longer turn his gaze elsewhere but keeps it fixed on the Lord. It is as though he is immersed in the vision of Christ. For us, Dante's anonymous Croatian has a name: he is the Servant of God, Alojzije Cardinal Stepinac, who was born a hundred years ago in Krašić and died on February 10, 1960. Truly this man, this Servant of God, kept his gaze fixed on Jesus, meditated on Jesus, lived in the vision of Christ, and thus was always conformed to Christ: he was transformed into Christ, being himself a living image of Christ suffering with the crown of thorns and with the wounds of his Passion.

The three readings of today's liturgy are in their way an image of Christ. About the Sermon on the Mount, from which we heard an excerpt (Lk 6:17, 20–26), the Holy Father in his encyclical *Veritatis splendor* (no. 16) says that it is a kind of hidden autobiography of Christ, because in reality Christ himself is that "poor man" who was born in the manger outside the city because there

---

[1] Dante Alighieri, *Paradiso* XXXI, 103.

was no room in the inns and died naked on the Cross, deprived of everything.

Christ was "hated", "excluded" (Lk 6:22), because he proclaimed God's love for all mankind. And thus, seeing and meditating on today's readings, we see Christ, but in this way we can also understand better the message of the Servant of God: the cardinal guides us to Christ and makes his message present, and Christ makes us see the profundity of the cardinal's heart, the true roots of his life.

I would like to call attention to two short passages from today's Gospel. First of all to the words already cited: "Blessed are you when men hate you, and when they exclude you and revile you, and cast out your name as evil." Our Blessed, the Servant of God, experienced precisely this contempt for human dignity, experienced solitude and suffering. We find a sort of prophetic anticipation of these words in Socrates—as reported by Plato in his *Apology* (31 c)—when before the tribunal he says: "No one who in the name of his conscience opposes a prevailing multitude will be able to save himself on this earth." Cardinal Stepinac was a conscientious man, who in the name of his conscience opposed the prevailing majorities. He was a man whose conscience was enlightened by the words of Christ, a man whose conscience was formed by the truth of Christ. And by means of this conscience, his journey led him to the truth: and it is the journey of true life. Because as a man shaped by a Christian conscience, he opposed totalitarianisms: thus, during the time of the Nazi dictatorship, he was a defender of the Jews, of the Orthodox, and of all who were persecuted; and then, during the time of Communism, he was the advocate of his faithful and of his murdered and persecuted priests. He became, above all, the advocate of God on this earth; he defended man's right to live with God; and he defended the presence and the position of God on this earth.

Cardinal Stepinac did not engage in politics. He respected the State as long as and to the extent to which it was an authentic State. In this he followed the maxim of Saint Ambrose, when he says: "I always showed the desired and proper deference to the emperors, but the things of God are not mine, they are not the emperor's; they are things of God, and I must respect and defend what is God's."[2] And this is exactly what Cardinal Stepinac did: he defended the things of God against man's false, mistaken omnipotence; he defended God's rights and, thus, true human rights, the true image of man against totalitarianism, which does not acknowledge the power of God, does not acknowledge the presence of God, the rights of God in the world.

The Servant of God was a conscientious man but, in all his admirable steadfastness, was never a hard man, never became bitter, much less experienced hatred, because he defended the truth, because his conscience was immersed in the face of Christ, had been shaped by Christ. This steadfastness was at the same time love for his fellowmen, love even for his persecutors. And, thus, he teaches us that the steadfastness of the Christian conscience reconciles truth and love, because the conscience is a union of truth and love. Being a conscientious man, he overcame evil with good and transformed evil with his invincible love, nourished by the love of Christ.

The other sentence on which I would like to dwell is the first of the beatitudes: "Blessed are you poor, for yours is the kingdom of God" (Lk 6:20). What does "blessed" mean? Of what does this beatitude or blessedness consist? Clearly this blessedness does not consist of earthly happiness in the banal sense of well-being, success, career, having everything, being able to do everything. It is

---

[2] Ambrose, *Lettera fuori coll.* 10, 1.12.

understood in just the opposite sense. It is, instead, what Saint Paul tells us today in the Reading: "If Christ has not been raised," if we have only this life and this time, "we are of all men most to be pitied" (1 Cor 15:17, 19). And truly the Servant of God lived and suffered this mystery of faith, this exclusion, this solitude. He suffered misery, but he was able to endure this misery because behind the misery he found true blessedness. He was able to say: "I know that my Redeemer lives." He knew that in the future he would live with his Redeemer.

Consequently, of what does this beatitude, this being blessed, consist? It is not something of this world; it is a reality of God, a divine truth, a truth in God for man that will be revealed to each one in his time, when God calls him Home. And whoever wants to live this beatitude, to arrive at this blessedness, cannot be closed off in himself, but must instead extend beyond himself, must go out of himself, must live in overcoming himself, must abandon himself completely into God's hands. It is by losing himself that one truly experiences the place of true beatitude.

We know how the Servant of God truly lived in this overcoming of self. He did not consider his episcopal office, his priesthood, as a prestige, a distinction. Truly he lost himself in God and, in losing himself, found true life. Therefore, it was precisely by abandoning himself that he became free: free from human honors, free to endure all affronts and calumnies, free to love.

In light of this true blessedness, we can understand also these other words of Jesus: "Woe to you that are rich, for you have received your consolation" (Lk 6:24). Whereas the man is blessed who lives, not for himself, but, so to speak, outside of himself, who lives with his gaze turned to God, stretched out to God, and oriented toward God, who entrusts himself into God's hands, the rich man in contrast wants to have everything for himself, wants to possess life, wants to possess himself, closes himself off, wants to have success in all the things of this world. And nevertheless, in truth, in possessing all that wealth, he becomes impoverished, because he becomes poor in the true reality that is found with God; and his life—as today's First Reading says—becomes "like a shrub in the desert" (Jer 17:6), "like chaff which the wind drives away" (Ps 1:4) because he is empty. A life like that, an "I alone" like that, is not sufficient, because it is a life devoid of truth, devoid of love, because it does not know God. Therefore Jesus' words, "Woe, for you have received your consolation", are not an external vendetta, as it might seem at first. They are only the revelation of what happens when someone closes himself off in matter, in the things of this world, when someone wants to have himself for himself alone and lives only for himself.

Thus we see how the words of the Gospel coincide with the First Reading and with the psalm, the Responsorial Psalm for this Sunday, in which the prophet, prefiguring Christ and his testimonies, says: "Blessed is the man who trusts in the Lord.... He is like a tree planted by streams of water", which extends its roots toward the stream and will never lack water (Jer 17:7–8; Ps 1:3). We find this water that will never fail, that gives eternal life to that tree, in the faith of the Church, in the Word of God. God himself gives us this water. In interpreting Psalm 1, Augustine says: the man blessed by the prophet in the psalm is like a tree that has roots extended upward, that has roots in heaven and grows toward heaven. Thus, in the world's view, he appears to be lost and seems like a stranger on earth, but in reality he has sunk his roots into the true water of life. Cardinal Stepinac truly was a tree like this, growing upward toward communion with God, and thus he seemed to be almost beyond the world, like a stranger in the world. Truly he planted his roots where the water of true life is found.

The Psalm, the Reading, and the Gospel invite us, therefore, to consider the authentic Either-Or: either live alone through this time on earth, only for oneself, and be *apparently* happy, or else live with God, for God, and thus for others. There is no other choice. A third possibility does not exist. The Servant of God showed us the true path of life and invites us also to be strong and steadfast, to have the courage to live in conflict with the world when the world conflicts with the Word of God. Someone who lives that way knows very well that ultimately only the Word of God lives and is valid and that this is the true reality.

In 1934, when the Servant of God was elected Archbishop-Coadjutor of Zagreb, he was terrified. He knew very well the difficult situation of the Catholic Church and of the Catholic faithful in his country, in a Yugoslavia that in the aftermath of World War I the Allies had created artificially by joining contrasting elements in a strongly anti-Catholic mold. But he was aware not only of this difficulty, this threat: he knew also the strength of the totalitarian, atheistic ideologies, which at that time were already strong and that would increasingly determine everything. In this situation, he could not consider the episcopate as a promotion in the human sense, as a higher step in a human career. He knew that the episcopate at that moment was a sacrifice, a loss of self: a surrender into God's hands.

He expressed the program of his episcopate, of his life, in these words: *In Te Domine speravi*. "In You, O Lord, I have trusted." This is his episcopal motto, which coincides with the words of today's First Reading: "Blessed is the man who trusts in the LORD, whose trust is the LORD" (Jer 17:7). *In Te Domine speravi.*

He entrusted himself to the Lord in great suffering, he entrusted himself to the Lord knowing that in the Lord is the water of true life, that true happiness is found in the Lord. In difficulties, he remained a man of hope, because he was a man of faith and, thus, a man of love for his neighbor, a man of true love.

Today Cardinal Stepinac invites us to this courage, invites us to place our trust in Christ, to be men and women of hope.

"In you, O Lord, I have placed my hope." Someone who lives by these words knows that the final words of the *Te Deum* are true also: *non confundar in aeternum,* "Let me never be confounded."

# WHEN A MACHINE IS BLESSED

*Gen 1:1–31*

The blessing of tractors has already become a fine tradition of this country. But someone might object: What does it mean to bless a machine? A blessing does not help a machine to function; a tractor is a product of technology, and the conditions for its functioning are the laws of mechanical construction, nothing else. Someone who speaks this way is partly correct, but only partly. Of course a blessing is no substitute for the correct mechanical construction or for the safe operation of a machine. But the machine is not a self-enclosed world; the machine has its origin in an idea and in a human will, and it serves a definite purpose; the tractor, for example, assists the work of the farmer, assists him in his task of subduing the earth according to the Creator's words: "Fill the earth and subdue it; and have dominion ... over every living thing" (Gen 1:28). A machine is part of human work; it is an instrument of our labor. To bless a machine, therefore, means to bless our work, to place our work into God's hands. The machine represents your work, and the blessing is a prayer, in the name and in the power of the Church, that God may be with you day by day in your diligent efforts to provide our daily bread, the fruit of the earth, which is always a gift of God's goodness and the product of our labor.

Thus we can say: a machine depends on man and on his ingenuity, but man depends on God. Machines, all technical inventions, can be either a blessing or a curse for mankind, and today we see more and more this ambiguity of modern technology. Thus, technology is good or bad, just as man himself is good or bad. When man loses himself, his domination of the earth becomes the destruction of the earth. When man loses himself, his technological abilities become a direct threat to the survival of the human race. Man loses himself when he forgets his Creator, God. In forgetting God, he can no longer decipher the message of his nature, he forgets his own measure and becomes for himself a riddle without an answer. When we forget God, things become mute, they are merely material with which to make something, but without a reason why, devoid of all deeper significance. If we return to God, things start to speak. Scripture gives us two images for a true domination of the earth: the garden and the holy city. The garden expresses a mutual friendship between earth and man, the harmony of creation. When man is upright, the earth gives its fruit, the earth becomes a garden and a fatherland.

The blessing of tractors is a prayer that our work may be in God's hands, scaled to God and to his goodness; a prayer that, through our work, the earth might increasingly become a garden and a fatherland; a prayer that our work and our use of the machines will not destroy but, rather, build up the earth, build up a human world and prepare for the future city, the future garden of the Kingdom of God. The blessing of tractors is, furthermore, an acknowledgment of the fact that even today man's life ultimately depends, not on machines, but on God's goodness. The fruit of the earth comes from him even today; we ourselves depend on him, and where he is not present, our power becomes a curse; where there is no God, nothing remains good. Thus, the blessing becomes also an examination of conscience, an admonition: to live in harmony with God, to work in union with his will.

Our human work, represented in these machines, serves, first of all, our earthly life: it prepares our daily bread for us. But just as man goes beyond the whole material world, so too our work has a higher dimension than merely assuring bodily life. Our work is always necessarily collaboration; one person needs the other, and the machine also represents this interdependence: we do not begin at zero—others have thought and worked for us and, thus, work with us; our work prepares our food. By working, we live, one person thanks to another; work creates community, creates the garden and the city. To work is to humanize. But this is not yet all. Work for natural bread also prepares the supernatural bread and, thus, extends also to the preparation for eternal life. The liturgy of the Church, in its prayer over the offerings, points out this mystery to us, this higher destination of our work: "Blessed are you, Lord God of all creation, for through your goodness we have received the bread we offer you: fruit of the earth and work of human hands; it will become for us the bread of [eternal] life." Our work and God's goodness meet in the gift of the earth, in the bread and wine. Our work becomes Eucharist. God's goodness creates bread from our work; the same goodness—in response to our prayer—transforms the earthly bread into food of eternal life, changes it into the Body of Christ. Thus, we see the value of work and of prayer. By walking together, we create a new earth. Our work prepares for the presence of Christ, becomes food of eternal life. Even a machine, the instrument of our work, does not remain foreign to Christian life. Embraced by prayer, it can become an instrument of blessing and help to prepare the future city. Let us pray that God in his goodness may bless our work.

# "ONLY HE WHO EXPERIENCES THE ABSURD IS ABLE TO CONQUER THE IMPOSSIBLE"

## (Miguel de Unamuno)

*May 19, Feast of Saint Josemaría Escrivá*
*Rom 8:26–30; Lk 5:1–11*

The mysterious Book of Revelation by Saint John terrifyingly speaks to us about the past and the future of our history, yet continuously tears the veil that separates heaven and earth, showing us that God has not abandoned the world. However great evil may be in certain moments, in the end God's victory is certain.

Amid earth's tribulations, we can still hear a louder song of praise. Around God's throne there is a growing choir of the elect, whose lives—spent in self-forgetfulness—have now been transformed into joy and glorification. This choir does not sing only in the next world; it is prepared in the middle of history, while remaining hidden from it. This is made quite clear by the voice that comes from the throne, that is, from God's seat: "Praise our God, all you his servants, you who fear him, small and great" (Rev 19:5). This is an exhortation to do our own part in this world, thus beginning to belong to the liturgy of eternity.

The beatification of Josemaría Escrivá tells us that this priest of our [twentieth] century is in the choir of those who praise God, and that the words of today's Reading pertain to him: "Those whom he justified he also glorified" (Rom 8:30). Glorification is not only something in the future; it has already happened: and beatifications remind us of this.

"Praise our God, all you his servants,... small and great" (Rev 19:5). In this voice, which in the Book of Revelation issues from the throne, Josemaría Escrivá saw his vocation, but he did not refer and apply it only to himself and to his life. He considered it his mission to transmit these words that come from the throne, to make them audible in our century. He invited the great and the small to give praise to God, and precisely in this way he himself gave praise to God.

Josemaría Escrivá became aware very early of the fact that God had a plan for him, that he was supposed to dedicate his life to a task. But he did not know what this task was. How, then, could he find an answer? Where could he look for it? He set out to search, above all, in listening to the Word of God, Sacred Scripture. He read the Bible, not as a book from the past, not even as a book of problems to debate, but as a present word that speaks to us today, as a word in which *we* appear, each of us, and in which we must seek our place in order to find our path.

In this search, he was moved particularly by the story of Bartimaeus, the blind beggar sitting along the road to Jericho who heard Jesus passing and started to cry out in a loud voice for his mercy (Mk 10:46–52). While the apostles tried to silence the blind beggar, Jesus turned to him with the question, "What do you want me to do for you?" And Bartimaeus' answer was: "Master, let me receive my sight."

Josemaría recognized himself in Bartimaeus. "Master, that I may see!" was his constant prayer: "Let me know your will for me." Man truly sees only when he learns to see God; and one begins to see God only when one sees the will of God and is willing to consent to it. The true driving force of Escrivá's life was and remained the desire to see God's will and to put his own will in God's. "Thy will be done on earth as it is in heaven" (Mt 6:10). Through this desire, through this incessant prayer, he was prepared, when the moment of illumination arrived, to respond as Peter did: "Master, ... at your word I will let down the nets" (Lk 5:5).

And his Yes was no less daring and adventuresome than the Yes pronounced then by Peter on the Sea of Galilee, after an unsuccessful night of fishing: Spain was steeped in hatred against the Church, against Christ, against God. Some wanted to eradicate the Church from Spain, when the task of casting the nets for God was given to him. But as God's fisherman, he let down the nets tirelessly throughout his life, into the waters of our history, in order to draw the great and the small to the light, so that they might see.

The will of God. Paul says to the Thessalonians: "This is the will of God, your sanctification" (1 Thess 4:3). The will of God is ultimately quite simple and, in its main point, is the same for everyone: sanctity. And, as today's Reading tells us, sanctity means being conformed to the image of Christ (Rom 8:29). Josemaría Escrivá considered sanctification not only as a personal vocation but, above all, as a task for others: to instill the courage for sanctity, to gather for Christ a community of brothers and sisters. The word "saint" had undergone a dangerous reduction over the course of time, which is in effect even today. We think of the saints depicted over the altars, we think of miracles and heroic virtues, and we think that this is something reserved to a few elect persons, among whom we cannot be numbered. In this way, we leave sanctity to those few unknown souls, and we are content to be as we are. Josemaría Escrivá shook people out of this spiritual apathy:

"No, sanctity is not the exception, but the usual thing, the
normal thing for every baptized person. It does not consist of inimitable heroic deeds, but has a thousand forms;
it can be achieved everywhere and in every profession. It
is normalcy. It consists of this: living your usual life with
your sights set on God and shaping it in the spirit of faith."
For this mission, the Blessed traveled tirelessly on several
continents and spoke to the people in order to instill in
them the courage for sanctity, that is, for the adventure
of being Christians, wherever life has placed us. Thus he
became a great man of action, who lived by the will of God
and called others to the will of God, but without becoming a moralist. He knew that we cannot justify ourselves;
thus, just as love presupposes the passivity of being loved,
so too sanctity is always associated with a passive element:
agreeing to be loved by God. His foundation is called *Opus
Dei*, the Work of God, not *Opus nostrum*, "our work".
Josemaría Escrivá's work is not an attempt to create some
work *of his own*: he did not intend to build a monument to
himself. "My work is not mine", he could and intended to
say, conforming himself to Christ (cf. Jn 7:16): he did not
want to do his own work, but, rather, he wanted to give
God room to accomplish His work. Certainly he was also
well aware of the words that Jesus addresses to us in the
Gospel of Saint John: "This is the work of God—faith"
(cf. Jn 6:29)—that is, to hand oneself over to God, so that
he can act through us.

    In this way, a further identification with another
Gospel phrase comes about: with the words of Peter in
today's Gospel that become his words: "Homo peccator
sum," (I am a sinful man) (Lk 5:8). When our Blessed
became aware that his life was an abundant catch of fish,
he was terrified—like Peter—by his littleness compared to
what God wanted to do with him and through him. He

described himself as a "founder without a foundation" and
an "inadequate instrument"; he knew and saw very well
that he was not the one who did all that, that he was not
able to do it; instead, it was God who acted through an
instrument that seemed completely inadequate. And ultimately this is what is meant by "heroic virtue": what happens is something that only God himself can do. Josemaría
Escrivá recognized his own misery, but he abandoned
himself to God without considering himself. Without asking questions about himself and about what was his own,
he placed himself at God's disposal in order to carry out his
will. He himself always spoke about his "foolish actions":
about beginnings without any material means whatso-
ever, about beginnings in the realm of impossibility. They
seemed to be foolish actions, which he had to dare and did
dare to undertake. The words of his great Spanish compa-
triot Miguel de Unamuno come to mind: "Only fools act
seriously, the clever accomplish only nonsense."

He dared to be something like a Don Quixote of God.
Does it not seem rather quixotic to teach, in today's world,
humility, obedience, chastity, detachment from possessions, altruism? God's will was for him true reasonableness,
and so gradually the reasonableness of what was apparently
irrational was able to come to light.

God's will. The will of God has a concrete place and
form in this world. it has a body. In his Church, Christ
remained a body. And hence obedience to God's will is
inseparable from obedience to the Church. Only if I bring
my own mission into the obedience of the Church can I
be sure that I am not mistaking my own ideas for God's
will but am truly following *his* call. Therefore, obedience
to the hierarchical Church and unity with her was for
Josemaría Escrivá always the fundamental criterion of his
mission. In this there is no authoritative positivism: the

Church is not a system of power; she is not an association for religious, social, or moral purposes that she devises by herself and that eventually she can exchange for others more in step with the times. The Church is a sacrament.

This means that she does not belong to herself. She does not carry out her own work but must be at the service of God's work. She is bound to God's will. The sacraments are the authentic scaffolding of her life. The center of the sacraments, however, is the Eucharist, in which this corporeal character of Jesus touches us most directly. Thus, for our Blessed, ecclesiality meant, above all, life centered on the Eucharist. He loved and proclaimed the Eucharist in all its dimensions: as adoration of the Lord, corporeally present among us; as a gift in which he continues to offer himself to us; as a sacrifice, in keeping with the words: "Sacrifices and offerings you have not desired, but a body have you prepared for me" (Heb 10:5; cf. Ps 40:6–8). Christ can be distributed only because he sacrificed himself, because he accomplished the exodus of love and offered and still offers himself. We become conformed to the image of the Son (Rom 8:29) only if we enter into this exodus of love, only if we become an offering: there is no love without the passive of the Passion, which transforms us and makes us open.

When Josemaría Escrivá was two years old and in danger of death—the doctors had already given up on him—his mother decided to consecrate him to Mary. Amid unspeakable hardships, by difficult pathways, she finally brought the child to the Marian Shrine in Torreciudad to entrust him to the Mother of the Lord, so that *she* might become his mother. Thus, for his whole life, Josemaría Escrivá was conscious of being under the mantle of the Mother of God, who was a mother to him. In his office, facing the door, stood the image of Our Lady of Guadalupe;

every time he went into that room, his first glance fell on that image. It was the last thing he saw, too. At the hour of his death, he was able to enter his room and look up at our Lady's image just before death overtook him.

While he was dying, the bells were tolling for the Angelus, the announcement of Mary's *fiat* and of the grace of the Incarnation of her Son, our Savior. Under this sign, which stood at the beginning of his life and always guided it decisively, he also returned Home. Let us thank the Lord for this contemporary witness to the faith, for this tireless herald of his will, and let us pray: "Master, that I may see. Grant that I, too, may know and do your will."

# ON THE WAY
# TO THE LAND OF THE FUTURE

*Gen 14:17–20*

Through the words of the Reading that we heard first, from the obscurity of distant history, the figure of Melchizedek, the priest of Salem, appeared in our midst as though to stand together with us at the table of the Lord, to accompany together with us the procession of the peoples toward Christ. This figure makes clear once again and more profoundly the fundamental idea that was our point of departure today: *Corpus Christi* as the feast of God's hospitality, to which many are called from the North and from the South, from the East and from the West. He illustrates the two inseparably necessary aspects of hospitality: the spiritual-religious aspect and the corporeal one. Melchizedek was a priest, but he did not belong to the lineage of Abraham or to his religion. Spiritually, too, he was a foreigner to him. Nevertheless, Abraham recognizes in this priest of God Most High the same faith that became the guiding star of his life, also; he recognizes a common call and a common following. Thus in Melchizedek we encounter a truly ecumenical figure. Against the fanaticism of ideologies, against the self-inflicted hardening of heart that leads religious communities into fanaticism, he embodies the great breadth of faith that embraces all those who seek what is eternal and strive to shape the world in terms of it. These two men, Abraham and Melchizedek, could be a summons to us in this hour, to all who seek God in our time, to accept one another, to support each other in our common search for the eternal; to oppose the common decline into materialism, albeit in so many forms and under different names, in a single effort to stand together, with the heartfelt generosity that springs from standing together with God. Abraham gave to this foreign priest a tithe, as though he were one of his own people. In the Old Covenant, the prerogatives of the priest were similar to those of the stranger and of the poor person. Everyone knew that the encounter with God occurs in persons of this type; that by means of the stranger, the poor person, and the priest, God wishes to enter into this world. The Old Testament shares an aboriginal conviction of mankind that God might sit down at my table in the stranger. My relation with God may be determined in my encounter with the stranger. In fact, in Melchizedek, a precursor of Jesus Christ appears in the presence of Abraham.

I think that this reminder is of the greatest possible concern to us, in a country with problems pertaining to foreign workers and asylum seekers, with problems pertaining to coexistence between foreigners and natives. Certainly some migrants request asylum for the wrong reasons, the pursuit of material well-being. But for those who really need our help, there must always be room. In all the poor, the suffering, and the persecuted, Christ the Lord is the one who continues to knock at our door. So we must not insist hardheartedly on what is ours and show hostility toward foreigners. Being Christian is manifested precisely in openness to one another, in mutual acceptance, in the willingness to grow together and to receive from each other.

Let us return to Melchizedek. According to a very ancient Christian tradition, the Old Testament participates in the feast of the New. Our Corpus Christi procession has always been intended as a participation in the great pilgrimage of the peoples toward the Eternal. In the great Corpus Christi procession in Munich in 1582, for example, fifty-nine biblical scenes and almost four thousand persons were depicted, practically the entire Old and New Testament. The whole history of salvation traveled through the streets of our city. Certainly, such an extravagant presentation is an expression also of the theatrical sensibility and taste for tableaus that was typical of that era. But the real motive that comes to light here is part of the original deposit of the Christian faith and of the Eucharistic faith. In the Roman Canon, the First Eucharistic Prayer of the Holy Mass, we pray that God may accept our sacrifice as he was willing to accept the sacrifice of Abel, the sacrifice of Melchizedek, the sacrifice of Abraham. Abel, Melchizedek, and Abraham represent three eras of the history of religions and of human history to which we are united in the Eucharist.

Of course, this poses the question of whether such prayer is truly correct; whether it is not opposed to the definitive character of Christ's sacrifice; whether it does not disregard the absolute and complete sufficiency of what he did, by trying once again to set up human works alongside of it; whether it is not an attempt to go back before him to an earlier time, to the Old Covenant.

To find an answer, let us take a closer look at these three figures. Abel is the one who sacrifices the lamb, but then he himself is sacrificed, becoming a "lamb" (cf. Gen 4:3-8). In him already shines the mystery of the one who became the Lamb of God in this world. In Abel, humanity goes to meet Christ and Christ comes to meet us. And for this reason, the Canon of the Mass also attributed to him two titles of Christ: "puer iustus" (servant of God, which can also mean child of God) and "the just man".

Beside Abel, we see Melchizedek today. His name means "king of justice". His place of origin is noted as

Salem, which means "peace". Melchizedek is the "king of justice" who lives in the place of peace and offers to God bread and wine, the gifts of creation, as a thanksgiving for creation. Through him is manifested again the one who is the true King of the universe; the one who established God's justice in our midst and whose place is peace. Peace is an ancient term for the Eucharist, the place in which Christ reigns and brings mankind into the peace of God. Manifested through Melchizedek is the one who turned bread and wine, the gifts of creation, into the sign of his presence in our midst, because he himself is the grain of wheat that died, the grapes that were trodden and became wine. So, once again, in Melchizedek, man goes to meet Christ and Christ comes to meet us.

And then there is Abraham. His own sacrifice consists of his willingness to offer, in his son, his future, to deprive himself of a future, to place his future in God's hands (cf. Gen 22:1–19). If we reflect that in those days it was thought that man's immortality, his future, consisted of living on in his descendants, then Abraham, in his son, gave away the promise that he had received, his blessing; he gave himself away. This man, too, who in giving his future gave himself, points to the future Lamb, who would give himself in sacrifice. Abraham's whole journey was a journey toward the future Lamb. Again in him, Christ, the Lamb of God, is manifested.

This brief retrospect shows us that the Roman Canon does not place arbitrary figures beside Christ. It shows, instead, how Christ traverses all of history, how he, throughout history, goes to meet man, and how in all ages there are men who are his pathway through time. In all of them, the procession of the peoples toward the Lord takes place.

Thus Abel, Melchizedek, and Abraham illustrate what the Corpus Christi procession is. The Corpus Christi procession represents what we are: people of God on pilgrimage toward the land of the future. And the Church, in turn, represents what humanity is, what history is: being on a journey toward future things, being on a journey to meet the Lord who created the world and calls it to become his kingdom. Certainly in the Old Covenant there is something old and in the New something new as compared to the old. Over the figures of the Old Covenant, about whom we spoke, still hovers a certain unsatisfied desire, indeed, a certain sadness, if we think of murdered Abel, if we think of Abraham's look of expectation. They all stretch out their hands toward the future and invoke it before it is there.

The celebration of the Eucharist, however, means that God's response is presence. The celebration of the Eucharist means that Christ enters and says: *Ecce adsum*, "I am present." He, who is the land of the future, already stands in our midst. Our journey no longer goes toward something indefinite; rather, it goes toward him who is already here. For this reason, the Eucharist of the New Covenant is a feast of joy, and we can complete our procession toward the future land as joy and thanksgiving. Christ, however, precedes us. Therefore, we, too, are still on pilgrimage, included in the procession of the great wayfarers toward the eternal. With them, we journey toward the eternal, so that God's kindly face might shine upon us, as the prayer of the Canon says.

Abel, Melchizedek, and Abraham each contribute something of their own to our understanding of the mystery of Christ. Yet they have a common message, too, which in Berlin was once the motto of the 1980 *Deutscher Katholikentag* [General Assembly of German Catholics]: "The love of Christ is stronger." Abel is stronger than Cain. *Love* abides and conquers, not violence. This is the great profession of faith that we make today with the sacrificed Lamb, with the true Abel, with the crucified and risen Christ, and that gives us the courage, even in the midst of a world of violence, nevertheless, to be thankful, happy people. Love is stronger than violence. Violence is never constructive. There is no end that could justify violence as a means. Someone who uses violence to build the future remains a violent man without respect for human dignity. In other words, he has thrown away precisely what ought to be our future. There is only one means that is in itself an end: love. Therefore, we are "demonstrating" with Abel against Cain. In this time of violence, let us side with Abel, with Jesus Christ, and let us profess that Christ's love is stronger, that it is the land of the future.

The love of God is our way and our destination. This is true not only about relations between foreigners and natives; it is true also about our own relations with one another. How much loneliness there is among us, even within our families; how much loneliness in the young people who have no one to speak with about their needs and who feel that no one understands them; how much loneliness among the sick, among the elderly; how much loneliness and lack of communication between the generations; how much loneliness among the dying. Our journey, our procession should continue toward all of them when we go our separate ways today. The paths leading to them are and ought to be our everyday paths; our path with Christ toward the Father, as represented today in the way that we have in common. In this faith, let us walk with Christ.

# JESUS AND THE FAITH OF
# THE LITTLE ONES

*Mk 5:21–43*

This passage from the Gospel conveys two fundamental messages: in the first place, it is situated in a cycle of miracles, the main point of which, however, is not the miracles themselves so much as the one who performs them, Jesus of Nazareth. In this sense, we ought to say more correctly that it is situated in a Christological cycle that is supposed to show clearly to those listening to the Gospel who this Jesus is. It is a matter of making him recognizable, of leading to the knowledge of Jesus Christ.

And the matter does not end there; Jesus interests us, not merely as any other historical personage might, but rather as the one in whom it becomes clear who God is. In this sense, the Christological cycle, from the perspective of the Gospel itself, is a theological cycle, precisely because Jesus is not a self-enclosed man at all but, rather, in this cycle the complete man who is really worth knowing, the man who is open by definition, through whom and in whom one can know who God is.

That this is so is evident precisely from the fact that we are situated here within a crescendo of miracles. We find ourselves confronting the first great climax of the Gospel, which, with the resurrection of a dead person, is also intended as a prelude to the Resurrection of the Lord. Here the Gospel shows him to us, on the one hand, as the

One who has power over death, as the One in whom man's fallen condition—his real misery—is overcome, as the One who is salvation, as the One in whom the new creation takes place, in whom God the Creator comes to meet us; and, at the same time, as the One who, by passing through death in the Resurrection, brings to fulfillment what is only suggested here as a prelude.

In the second place, we must add that, although indeed the cycle of miracles allows us to recognize him in this way through these events—which is to say, as the One who is going toward death and Resurrection and who is therefore the power of God in the world—he is not simply placed in front of us; rather, a relation between us and him must be created, it must be demonstrated what he is for us and how we can reach him. In this sense, we can say that the text is also a catechesis on faith, which tells us who we are and, at the same time, is meant to be an orientation precisely by showing his way, the Lord himself.

First, in the foreground of the narrative, is this element: the catechesis on faith and the orientation that it gives us. As the story unfolds, there is a sick woman who accosts him anonymously in order to be cured (Mk 5:25–34).

The scant information that the Gospel provides does not allow today's reader to recognize the extent of her need and, therefore, the depth of this process and also the claim that it contains. The reader must take into account the fact that, because of her illness—the flow of blood— the woman was unclean under the Law. Impurity, in turn, meant exclusion not only from human relations but also from a relation with God. This illness excluded her from the human community and, above all, made her unable to worship. This means that the person in that condition could not take part in the community in which people draw near to God. Consequently, because of this excommunication, which is social but extends to the relation with God, she is not only economically ruined, as we learn from the account; not only is the woman physically stricken and tormented, but she is wounded in her humanity, being excluded from human coexistence and from communion with God, and no one can help her. She is avoided; she is marginalized.

That being said, we can understand why she now makes one last attempt. She hears about a man from whom a healing power is said to issue, and, in order to be cured, she decides to touch him secretly and "incognito" (which in this case means: transgressing the limits imposed by the norms of ritual purity and, therefore, violating the Law even more). It happens that she is cured and, therefore, in the cultic sense, too, is once again clean, and the decisive relation of communion with God and with people is reestablished.

At this point, the account tells us that Jesus does not simply let her go away anonymously. That woman must know *who* cured her. An almost magical ancestral faith, which without much knowledge simply aims at contact and the strength that is found in it, must become true faith (cf. Mk 5:34). It must not remain merely an anonymous event; where Jesus appears, he adds the word. It is not simply the mere ritual, the mere action; instead, the cure that he grants is put into a spiritual context, with the word it is made open to thanksgiving, also. And only when she knows whom she has believed, only when her natural confidence in a power that acts upon her has become *faith in Jesus*, only then is she truly healed, as the Gospel says.

What happened here? Jesus with sovereign freedom transcended the norm of ritual purity. He is neither frightened nor alarmed by the fact that after such a contact he, too, is impure now, nor does he challenge it. He is free for the human being who is seeking and who is in need and

suffering, whose need matters more than the irreproach-
able character of the national and religious *status* of his
society. Through his freedom, he welcomed the marginalized, downtrodden woman back into the human community. To put it in modern terms, he violated the societal
*taboo*, allowing the humiliated person to touch him, and
with the freedom and the power of goodness he shattered
the power of prejudice.

Thus, without it being said explicitly in the text, a fundamental feature of the life and activity of Jesus emerges.
The freedom of goodness that places human need and
humanitarian aid above the irreproachability of his own
way of life and of the regulations that he encounters: this
is a basic feature of what distinguishes Jesus and of what
characterizes Christian life that is based on him. We should
become aware of the fact that, in a society that apparently
breaks all taboos and, therefore, seemingly sets out on
Jesus' path, altogether unmentioned new taboos emerge
between persons and a recklessness that tries to defend
only itself; and therefore that it is necessary to recognize
and oppose this. What is happening here, of course, contains in itself an element of reform, of overcoming a hard-
ened legalism; but not in the sense that people make things
cheaper and easier for themselves, rather in the sense that
people risk more and give more, not less.

Another feature seems to me to lie in the fact that Jesus
does not stop at the physical cure that the woman receives,
but summons her, addresses her, confronts her with himself and with his word. It does not stop at the miracle, the
merely physical healing, but rather entails an encounter
with him that produces the decision for him, the acceptance of his word, taking a stance for him who is the Word.

I think that this, too, is something that greatly concerns us. Today we are very convinced that a faith that

overlooked earthly needs would not accomplish its task, and we get very intensely involved in addressing precisely those earthly needs, in considering the socio-political character of salvation, and we make efforts to improve human conditions. Certainly this, too, is part of the totality of salvation. But in doing so, we forget that man needs something more and that precisely this "something more" is meant to proceed from Jesus Christ; that man needs the word; that the word, meaning, is for him a reality, less within arm's reach, but no less decisive.

We ought to let this necessary connection that Jesus establishes remind us not to disdain the word, not to think that people are provided for if they all have something to eat and if they all have an adequate income. We should not let ourselves be pushed back to the Marxist idea of salvation, which is too reductive, much less to the capitalist idea of salvation, which is even more impoverished, but, rather, truly recognize that man, in order to be saved, needs more than to satiate his hunger and to satisfy his external needs and that we, in following Jesus, exist precisely to offer again and again this "something more" and to open hearts and minds to the word that gives meaning and to see this even as our central task.

Of course, we must also be continually and acutely aware of the prophetic task of recalling and striving for a comprehensive salvation. The point, however, is to respond to the hunger for the word or to reawaken it where it is covered with rubble.

We can make one further observation now. The woman suspects that in Jesus there is simply a power, and she wants to touch it; her faith is no doubt insufficient, and actually erroneous, one might say, but despite this, Jesus accepts it. In this erroneous and magical faith he perceives a yearning for salvation that is present in that distortion and accepts that poor, distorted yearning as a path to him on which salvation can happen.

I think that, in interpreting this passage, it is possible to formulate a sort of theology of world religions that does not need to downplay the insufficiency of their religious endeavors yet is resolute about the fact that, through this insufficiency, a faith that God can still recognize and accept is seeking its path. For if we see here the breadth and fullness of the Lord's tolerance—he glimpses something else in a faith of this sort (although from the theological perspective it is highly dubious), something that he accepts and affirms, causing salvation to spring from it—this should make us, too, a little more tolerant, more careful, and more cautious in our judgments.

This should also lead us to be ourselves more willing to respect the faith of the little ones when, regarded rationally, it appears to be pre-critical and insufficient and to have respect for the yearning that is found in it. We should try to accept it, to develop it, and to bring it to completion, as the Lord does.

On the other hand, if we are honest, we must say that our faith may be rationally adequate, yet often problematic and questionable in God's sight; it, too, is a very fragile endeavor that in God's sight must appear unserviceable, since it is presumably askew in many respects. In this sense, what the Lord does is useful for us all; it is at the same time a consolation and an exhortation. With our own faith we only grope our way with difficulty, so to speak, hardly seeing Jesus at all, yet striving somehow to clear a path through the crowd, through everything that distorts him, so as to be able to touch something that is his. The Gospel shows us that even in this wearisome and fragmentary groping there is something that the Lord can accept, that he can do something with, and that, despite all our inadequacy and inability, we need not fear, as long as there is still this yearning to see him truly, at least to touch his garment.

There are few more beautiful images of what faith is: the determined will, even if obstructed in many ways and distorted, to make one's way through the crowd to find the Lord, to touch him, to receive salvation from him.

The second part of the Gospel, which tells about the resurrection of a dead person, directs our attention more to the figure of Jesus. In the first part, it is the figure of the woman that actually stands in the foreground, and with her our approach, our groping toward him, but of course seen in relation to how *he* regards it and accepts it. Now we can observe how a humanity that is very close meshes with divine power over life and death.

On the one hand, there is no hint here of a Pantocrator [Ruler of all]; the one who encounters us is rather a man to whom we can still listen directly. The Gospel even preserves the Aramaic formula of the words that call the child back to life ["Talitha cumi" (Little girl, I say to you: arise)]. This is a very rare instance, and it echoes the profound impression that it made, something that was handed on in the community and by the testimonies beyond the linguistic boundaries of the Greek mission. Indeed, we get the impression that the excitement of that moment was so great that those words still ring in the ears of the chronicler and that here he makes us listen to Jesus in all his humanity, just as he spoke.

On the other hand, this humanity is joined to his lordship, which, in the first place, is shown in the fact that here, too, he transgresses the norm of ritual purity— anyone who touched the dead became unclean. But he knows that he is, after all, the one who is the Life, the one who for his part does not participate in the impurity of death but on the contrary purifies and enlivens the land of death. We truly have here a prelude of what is announced by the Cross and the Resurrection.

This unique interpenetration of divine power and profound humanity is evident once again when we read that Jesus awakens the girl and then orders them to give her something to eat (Mk 5:43); therefore, he thinks of the most immediate human needs, which in such a tremendous moment might seem terribly remote. I think that precisely this interweaving of concerns is very important for what the Gospel means, for the image of God that it transmits. This humanity of Jesus makes visible the face of the biblical God, who is powerful, good, distant, and at the same time very close, whose power is different from what we human beings consider power, whose transcendence is different from the way we think about the distance of kings and lords, whose power shows precisely that it is a power to be good, to help.

Thus we come across another important fundamental conviction of the Bible: the power of evil is not creative. It is not a kind of Anti-God that has and builds its own world. The power of evil is based on destruction. Being is God's Yes, and where this Yes is, he is, and where he is, this Yes is, because he is the Creator who gives life. This means that the Christian who sides with Jesus Christ is in principle a man of Yes who stands on the side of building up, on the side of hope, which is stronger than the forces of destruction.

# THE GENUINE MIRACLE
# IS GOD CRUCIFIED

*Mk 6:1–6*

This text, in the context of Mark's Gospel, concludes the cycle of miracles. We come to a situation in which miracles can no longer happen. Since this is the point at which the ascending line of Jesus' ministry is unexpectedly interrupted, in the structure of the Gospel this text occupies a prominent position, underscored also—and, indeed, deliberately—by the fact that this is the last time it refers to Jesus appearing in a synagogue (Mk 6:2).

For Mark, therefore, this episode signals the decisive rift between Jesus and Israel. That day saw the definitive failure of his continual and repeated attempts to make his people's worship of God the place of his revelation. From that day on, there was no going back to the synagogue for Jesus—despite his undoubted effort in favor of the synagogue, despite his diligence in making synagogue worship the place of his word. This process fails, inasmuch as the synagogue denies, "excommunicates" him, resulting in the rift between him and Israel.

We know that the rift of that moment remains to this day and, to this day, has remained one of the most painful wounds of humanity. In that apparently unimportant incident, which no historian had reason to record, a momentous decision in world history was made, to which none of the great political events of that time can be compared: that moment of pride and rejection is what indelibly defines history from then on.

Here we see, so to speak, the weight of a human decision. We see how a moment of pride can act destructively, can cut short an appeal, a possibility, a way of God, and how, basically, the hidden, politically inconspicuous decisions in which man silently sets himself up as the final arbiter of "yes" or "no", are precisely the forces that move history. In what is apparently insignificant, in the relation between man and God's message, the paths of the individual and the course of history are decided.

How does the event described here unfold in greater detail? According to the brief account handed down to us by Mark, the people of Nazareth had probably heard that their fellow countryman Jesus, a carpenter, had suddenly appeared as a rabbi and had even become a famous rabbi, whose message and whose miracles had aroused Messianic hopes. Naturally they wanted to hear him in their town, too, because there is a sort of pride in the fact that a local man had had that degree of success in his career, but then their skepticism was stronger. They were well acquainted with this Jesus and his family. Although others admired him, they knew who he was: a carpenter who no doubt had worked for many of them, too, in any case a man whom they knew and who, as they had convinced themselves a hundred times, was no different from them. In their view, it could only seem ridiculous to regard him as the Messiah. They wanted to listen to him once in their synagogue, but basically their reaction had already been decided in advance: with a disarming smile, they would show him that they already knew who he was and that they would not let themselves be impressed by an insignificant carpenter who presented himself as a rabbi. This arrogance looks down on others and already knows that there can be nothing special there, and, therefore, in reality it no longer listens.

In Luke's version, however, there is an additional element; namely, Luke omits in the text of Isaiah that Jesus explains the words about God's vengeance against the peoples and reports only the message of reconciliation (Lk 4:16–19). For them, this is a very grave scandal. Indeed, renouncing vengeance means renouncing the actual reward in God's salvation and promise. Salvation without vengeance would really be no salvation at all, for it was not worth the trouble. Why had their people suffered? Why had they been devout, if nothing happened to the others and all were reconciled?

This, in broad strokes, is the unfolding of the facts, as we are able to reconstruct them. We must recognize that reactions of this sort are altogether understandable, that basically we ourselves behave similarly, that we think we know people; or else we no longer listen, deep down, after hearing something for the umpteenth time; we no longer let it into our heart; we think that we already know how it will end and what the consequences will be.

And there is also the other fact, that salvation and Christianity interest us only if we get something specific out of it and, so to speak, there is a negative effect for the others. All this is part of us, and I think that everyone, thinking of his own reactions, can formulate it in even more concrete terms.

From then on, Christendom has generally condemned the inhabitants of Nazareth and the Jews as those who rejected the Messiah. And here the question must be asked: Do we really have that much reason to judge, to divide mankind from our perspective and to cut off those who ought to be subject to God's vengeance? Here we must ask: Are vengeance and irreconcilable differences not perhaps written large in the history of Christian nations, too, of Christian groups and in our own hearts? Do we not also oppose a God who has become too familiar, whom we think we already know, and from whom we no longer expect very much? Very concretely, do we not also oppose his Church, which has become for us a mere routine, when we say: "We have known this for ages; no salvation can come from this"? We ought to ask ourselves very practically whether we ourselves do not behave just like the people in Nazareth.

When we turn the question around in this concrete form, the real theme of the text and the center of Mark's Christology emerge, namely, the fact that God's power is manifested here in weakness and wishes to be recognized in it. Certainly, the Marcan Christology starts with miracles, with mighty acts in which the power of God the Creator is manifested in Jesus. But these mighty acts do not achieve anything: their sole effect is that the initial enthusiasm crumbles more and more and does not turn into a true decision in favor of Jesus Christ.

From this grand overture, the Gospel according to Mark moves more and more toward the final weakness, toward the Cross. The paradox of Mark's presentation is that, certainly, the miracles quickly arouse enthusiasm and a mood, but no aftermath, no faith. Only that final rift, the Cross, has the effect of making the Roman centurion say, representing the people: "Truly this man was the Son of God" (Mk 15:39). God who had become absolute weakness is the genuine miracle that creates a response.

Thus Mark tries to lead us to the Christian decision and, at the same time, show us how the real Christ before whom we are placed, the God who is the miracle that heals the world again, is not in the great, exciting acts of power but, in reality, is manifested only to the extent to which the sensational aspect diminishes and God's power comes to meet us in weakness. Marcan Christology, by leading increasingly away from the miracles, from the emotions and the enthusiasm of the crowd, into the abandonment of the Crucified Lord, presents this very thing to us as the real miracle in which the decisive event of world history occurs, in which man can begin to follow and to understand God.

With that, the Gospel makes a statement about the form of divine revelation: God reveals himself in what is insignificant, in what is not exciting from a worldly perspective, through the Cross. We are used to hearing this. But we have long since neutralized it: either by magnifying the Cross excessively on the theological level; or else, when we take it seriously, we are like the people of Nazareth; we become angry and say: "Why a message that is basically so miserable and sad? Why does the Good News not sound more joyful? Why is it not something splendid and grand that takes its place in the great course of history and in its triumphs? Why should we not perceive God in everything in the universe that is beautiful, great, and luminous? Why are we caged in this wretchedness? Is this truly the way that can be Good News for us?"

Nietzsche famously said: "What hath hitherto been the greatest sin here on earth? Was it not the word of him who said: 'Woe unto them that laugh now!'" (*Thus Spake Zarathustra*, IV, 16). Secretly, in reality, is this Christianity not the religion of the resentment of the little folk, of the petty people who cannot bear what is great and therefore divinize what is small and wretched? In order to engage the Gospel seriously, we ought to admit the extent to which the feelings of the inhabitants of Nazareth are ours, too, that basically we consider this God too little and we reject the idea that God's salvation could be this minuscule event of history that concerns us generation after generation and that we ourselves have proclaimed for a long time.

And we could broaden the horizon further to the experiences of each one of us when we witness the failings of the Church, when we ourselves experience how people no longer need Christianity and we wonder: Is this really still God's cause, the cause that deserves a lifetime commitment?

I think that the answer runs in two directions.

It is not at all true that only the Cross, only weakness is the place of God's revelation. Rather, we believe also in Jesus as Son of the Creator, in the God from whom creation comes. In this sense, it is absolutely valid for Christians, too, that whatever is great and beautiful is a revelation of God that we cannot and must not let anyone take away. On the contrary: part of being Christian should be to notice how in all the little, complicated, and miserable things of the world there is nevertheless also the beauty of creation, the splendor of the glory of God, which we should keep in mind, which we ought to see because it shows us something of God. In an era in which we are accustomed to seeing the world as a function of our work and considering it pragmatically as what can be utilized, we must absolutely reawaken in ourselves and in others the overall perspective, so as not to see just the functional potentialities, but to learn anew to see creation, the beauty of creation that is meant to make us happy, that is given to us so that we might see the splendor of God's glory in which he shows himself to us in many ways. This is proved also by the fact that the feast is an essential part of the Christian faith and that in the feast and in its beauty something of the beauty of God and of God's face appears to us.

Yes, Christianity is not a path of resentment that forces us to disregard what is beautiful; rather, it believes in the

God who is the Father of Jesus Christ and, therefore, believes in creation and in its beauty. But however true all this may be, the fact remains that this is not the sole revelation of God, or even the most central one.

We have truly come to know the universe, not only when we have gradually gained insight into the major laws of gravitation and the like, but when we have descended to the smaller things, the atom and the elementary particles. Only the knowledge of what is smallest has placed the whole thing into our hands, the power to threaten the universe and the potential to conquer the universe, even to build a man-made universe. Only by finding what is smallest—the world, so to speak, at its lowermost, tiniest point—have we grasped it in what are apparently its most minuscule and weakest aspects; only in this way have we reached its roots and been able to take it in hand: we have found the point that Archimedes sought, from which it is possible to move the world. We have found the greatest thing and made it our own only when we have found it in the smallest.

Thus far in our reflections, though, we have always remained in the sphere of matter. In his teaching about the three orders, Blaise Pascal pointed out the even more profound changes that are necessary in order for us to recognize what is truly great. Alongside the order of matter stands the order of the mind: the least among the intellects is greater than the entire material cosmos. And above the order of the mind stands the order of divine love, in whose apparent smallness alone one can perceive what is truly great. Only when we reach the depths that are manifested in Christ crucified, only then do we perceive what is greatest, what holds the world together, the genuine force that sustains the universe. Here, too, what is absolutely great is recognized only in the infinitely small. Only in God crucified, only in the God who became the least thing in his whole universe do we confront, so to speak, the elementary particles of reality that cause the universe to explode [in the Big Bang] and make up the whole thing. Only here do we confront the genuine power and recognize the nucleus of reality, which lies not in quantities but in this power that loves, down to the foundation of reality. Only here do we confront the all-inclusive power of divine love that enters into man the "worm" (cf. Ps 22:6) and, thus, supports the whole. And what is infinitely great can be disclosed to us only if we do not proudly reject this infinitely small one.

Thus, I think that the episode in Nazareth can give us a glimpse of the fundamental Christian decision, the ongoing task of opposing the obvious Nazarene complex and its superficiality—the Nietzsche complex—and of accepting God: not only in his greatness, but in his hiddenness, in which he, just like the smallest thing, is the force that can transform the world. To accept him, therefore, not only as the mighty God who rules over all, but as the God of reconciliation, the God who works, not through power, but through self-abasement (Phil 2:6–7), through what is smallest (this being true power), as the God who in sorrow and on the Cross leads us back to ourselves by referring us to what is smallest and most profound, as the God who reveals true joy to us precisely and only in this way.

Thus, we confront a task that is not to be finished, which, above all, is not to be resolved theoretically, but to which, instead, we must continually allow ourselves to be called as witnesses like this one, so that we might learn to descend beyond outward appearances into the depth of reality and, thus, slowly become capable of seeing God's greatness and of speaking about it to others.

# THE MAIN THING NEEDED
# TO PURIFY THE EMPOISONED
# AIR OF THIS WORLD

*Gen 18:1–33; Lk 10:38–42*

Saint Luke connects the Gospel for last Sunday about the Good Samaritan and today's Gospel about Martha and Mary by means of the little Greek word *poréuestai*, "to be on the way".

The Gospel about the Good Samaritan ends with the word "Go" (Lk 10:37). The Gospel about Martha and Mary starts with: "Now as they went on their way" (Lk 10:38). And therefore these two Gospels are connected by the idea of being on the way.

We recall also the overarching view of Saint Luke whereby the whole public life of the Lord unfolds "on the way", on the way toward Jerusalem, toward the Paschal Mystery, the mystery of our redemption on the Cross and in the Resurrection. And along this way, Jesus seeks our love, our willingness, our listening, and prepares us for the mystery of his presence, for the gift of his life.

And after Easter, the Gospel tells us once again: "[Jesus] is going before you to Galilee" (Mt 28:7). He continues to be on the way to Galilee, the Galilee of the world in which we must proclaim today—with him, by his grace—the Kingdom of God and prepare the world for his presence.

In this sense, the Lord goes before us to Galilee and with us on the way toward the New Jerusalem, the celestial

Jerusalem, heaven. And thus, in this connection between the two Gospels, the Lord shows us also the different dimensions of love of neighbor.

Although in the Gospel about the Good Samaritan, the external aspect of social action, of external, material aid, is most evident, in the Gospel about Martha and Mary, another dimension comes to light, the dimension of the presence of his word, the dimension of meditation and interiority.

These two Gospel readings together show us, furthermore, that love of neighbor and love of God are inseparable, that they must interpenetrate one another, that in love of neighbor there must always be love for God, too. We must give to the other not only material things; we must also give him God. Otherwise, we forget the essential thing, what is truly "needful" (Lk 10:42).

On the other hand, though, our neighbor must also be present in our love for God, because in our neighbor Jesus is the one who comes and asks for our hospitality. It seems to me that this is an important teaching, especially for our time.

Indeed, after the council, the idea became widespread that the content of the Gospel was social development, that it was necessary above all to do external, material things and that only afterward there might be time left for God ...

We see the consequences of that: even the missionaries no longer had the courage to proclaim the Gospel. They thought that their task now was to contribute to the development of the underdeveloped countries. Thus they forgot about God, with terrible consequences: the destruction of the moral foundations of those societies. A love of neighbor that forgets God forgets the essential thing.

Let us turn now to the Gospel about Martha and Mary. At first glance, it seems to be a simple human lesson about the essential dimensions of true hospitality. The Lord tells us: for true human hospitality, it is not enough to give food, external things. The true host gives more, must give to the other, above all, his time, be open to the other, give him a bit of himself, listen to him in order to be able to respond to his needs.

But in this teaching, which at first glance is purely human—which tells us that even in simple human hospitality it is necessary to give not only external things—we see the glint of a deeper reality: the need to be open, above all, to the essential thing, to the presence of God, in which he gives himself in his Word.

And in this teaching about the necessity of being open to the Lord, of sitting at the Lord's feet in order to enter into communion with him, the Lord speaks also to today's Church. Because the same problems that we encounter in Martha and Mary exist also in the Church today.

In reality, we perform the services of Martha. We do so many external things: there are meetings, commissions, synods, discussions, decisions, documents in abundance, there are pastoral programs and the like. Yes, many things are being done . . .

But maybe in this continual activity of Martha, which tries to prepare everything for the success of pastoral activity, we forget too much the dimension of Mary, we forget that this true availability for the Lord, for his Kingdom, demands much more than external actions alone; we forget that it demands above all our willingness to sit down at the feet of the Lord, in meditation, in listening to his Word, in which he gives himself.

In a letter from Saint Thérèse of Lisieux to her sister Céline, there is a very beautiful passage on this situation in the Church. Interpreting the figures of Martha and Mary, she says that, when Mary pours the precious perfume on the Lord's head, "the APOSTLES complained";

and she continues: "It is really the same for us [today]: the most fervent Christians, priests (and bishops) think that we are exaggerated, that we should serve with Martha instead of consecrating to Jesus the vessels of our lives with the ointments enclosed within them.... [W]hat does it matter if our vessels be broken since Jesus indeed is consoled and since, in spite of itself, the world is obliged to smell the perfumes that are exhaled and serve to purify the empoisoned air" (August 19, 1894).[1]

This statement—that the perfume that purifies the polluted air of this world comes from the broken vessels of our lives, from this dimension of Mary—is not only a profound theology of the contemplative life and of the life of the Church in general but also, it seems to me, a true and profound theology of the liturgy.

In the liturgy, we must also perform the service of Saint Martha, of course, we must prepare for the Lord the sacred atmosphere, offer him our preparations, rehearse the ceremonies and the singing properly, present the gifts of this world, the bread and the wine: all this is necessary, and it is also necessary to do it well.

But in the liturgy, unless there is also the dimension of Mary, the contemplative dimension of simply sitting at the Lord's feet (Lk 10:39), the essential thing is missing. In this sense, if the liturgy is truly "Marian", that is, if it imitates Mary's attitude of sitting at the Lord's feet and listening to his word in order to receive the gift of himself, if the liturgy is truly contemplative, then ultimately from this attitude comes the purification of the polluted air of this world. I think that the purification of

---

[1] Saint Thérèse of Lisieux, *General Correspondence*, vol. 2, *1890–1897*, trans. John Clarke, O.C.D. (Washington, D.C.: Institute of Carmelite Studies, 1988), LT 169, pp. 882–83.

the empoisoned air of today's world can come only from a truly "Marian" liturgy.

In this sense, both in today's First Reading about the apparition of the Trinity to Abraham (Gen 18:1–33) and in the Gospel, I find a profound view of the liturgy in its two dimensions.

In the Book of Genesis, Abraham generously offers his hospitality to the Triune God. He offers a calf, bread and cheese, washes the feet of his guests, gives of himself. But finally it is the Lord who gives him the one thing necessary, the essential thing, who gives him a son and, with the son, a future, hope, life.

It is the same in the Gospel: Martha offers good things to the Lord, offers him the gifts of her house, and Mary offers him her listening, her full availability. And finally the Lord is the one who not only gives his Word but gives himself in it.

This is the essential point of the liturgy: we offer our poor gifts, and we receive from the Lord's hands the gift, the one thing needful: his Body and Blood, eternal life, the Kingdom of God, redemption. Let us pray to the Lord that he might help us, that he might help the Church to celebrate the liturgy well, truly to sit at the Lord's feet so as to receive the gift of true life, the life that is essential and needful for the salvation of all, for the salvation of the world.

# THE CROSS: THE LOVE THAT
# GIVES ITSELF, TOTAL
# SELF-GIVING TO OTHERS

*Is 42:1–9; Mt 16:21–27*

With extraordinary frequency, during these days in mid-
September, the Church places the Cross before our eyes.
Yesterday, we celebrated the Exaltation of the Holy Cross;
today, the commemoration of Our Lady of Sorrows, a
feast that, during the terrible plague epidemic that raged in
Europe from 1347 to 1353 causing more than twenty-five
million deaths, arose like a groan from the depths of the
Church. And in the Reading we just heard, the vision that
sprang from the depths of the heart of suffering Israel, which
in the suffering of exile viewed itself as the scapegoat of
world history on which the blows of the powerful nations
around them rained down. In this situation, Israel considered
itself, though not uniquely, as the Servant of God who does
not reject sorrow but accepts it and, precisely by doing so,
becomes the salvation of the world. In today's Gospel, the
truth of this still-obscure vision is made plain to us: Christ,
the Son of God who was rejected by the high priests, the
elders, and the scribes and was handed over to the pagans to
be tortured and killed (cf. Mt 16:21). In reality, all this does
not correspond to the desires that we men cherish. Man
would like to have cheerful deities, if possible a religion of
stupefaction, diversions, and pleasure; and hence also the
fact that Christianity continually faces the same recurring

temptation to consider and to dismiss the Cross as a sort of embarrassing accident that in reality should not have been and ought not to be. Therefore, in celebrating the Eucharist, we must not forget that it cost Christ's death and that from it comes the fruitfulness that now consoles and unites people and gives them the certainty of a mercy greater than the suffering of this world.

In today's Gospel, Peter appears in a contradictory way. First, as spokesman of the believing Church, the man who first proclaimed in the name of all the fundamental profession of faith: "You are the Christ, the Son of the living God" (Mt 16:16). With that, the Church began, and thus he became the foundation stone of the Church. This profession of faith continues to be the genuine heart of Christianity, from which it draws its strength and its life, and it is also the heart of every Christian life. And however powerful the Church may be, however much money and influence she may have, if this profession of faith, if this profound Yes to Christ, if the life that comes from him as the Son of God were to dry up, then all the rest would very quickly collapse; and our Christianity itself would not continue to exist for long and could not have any strength if this center, this Yes to Christ as Son of God, were to be omitted. Peter, therefore, stands there as the foundation stone of the Church, as the spokesman of the believing Church of every age. But he represents also the conflict that runs through the Church herself and the believer himself, the misunderstandings and the temptations that threaten his faith. He said quite correctly: "You are the Christ, the king of this world through the grace of God." And, nevertheless, he imagines that this God-king is just like the kings of this world, only a little more powerful. This follows from the fact that he had imagined God himself, too, after the model of the powerful men of this world, only a little mightier. But that is precisely where he goes wrong.

At the moment when God moves into this world, he does not look like Emperor Augustus or King Herod, but is Jesus of Nazareth. At the moment when God becomes man, he is not like one of the powerful men of this world, but is a powerless, suffering man. When God moved, so to speak, into this world, he was not the ruler enthroned over the Mediterranean world—Augustus—but was the one who was crucified in the name of Emperor Augustus and over whose head the inscription was mockingly posted: "the King of the Jews" (Mk 15:26). This mockery was the truth, pure and simple, and the tragic thing is that man considers the truth simply as a mockery. This follows from the fact that God—quite the opposite of how we always imagine him—is not, so to speak, a powerful person who takes delight in himself, but is Trinity. This means that he is dedication, is self-giving. The Father: total self-giving to the Son; the Son who gives himself back in exchange. And in this fact that God is total dedication, there is then the circle of Trinitarian love and what is genuinely divine, the divine power absolutely. Corresponding to this is the fact that the Lord dies on the Cross with his arms outstretched: total dedication, total self-giving to others. The Cross does not contradict the dignity of the Son of God but, rather, is his image in this world, the image of self-giving love, which becomes powerless and thus becomes what is truly divine and holy.

I will put it another way: a religion is a vision of the world that, if it had nothing to say to people when they are suffering, would have nothing at all to say. Because if man is not able to suffer and his suffering has no meaning, then he is not able to live, either. And if he cannot accept his own suffering, neither can he accept the suffering of others, and then only what is useful and advantageous prevails, barbarity prevails in this world. Therefore, it was profoundly necessary that God should come to meet us as the one who suffers: hence, his salvific love flourishes among us. And today this ought to tell us that he is close to us especially in suffering and to tell us—who are well—that he awaits us in those who suffer.

On the Mount of Olives, when the Lord was seized with anguish—all the anguish of mankind—in the most outcast loneliness that has ever existed, an angel came from heaven to comfort him (cf. Lk 22:43). This comfort was not, so to speak, an anesthetic or a means of alleviating the pain; rather, it was the fact that the love that he needed in his suffering came to him, thus giving him the courage to face it. And God's consolations are always like this; God's angels always act this way. Because in the world the Cross remains the Cross; and it remains this way so that again and again we have to cry to him to have mercy on us, to show us that he is near, and to give us his help. Today's Collect prayer, exhorting us to call on the Lord and to cry out to him, reads: "O God, you created and govern the universe; look down upon us so that we might experience the power of your mercy and dedicate ourselves wholeheartedly to your service." You who govern, you who support the universe in your hands, you who have the responsibility for everything, turn and look at what is in your hands. You are the Creator of us all; we are your creation, your children; look at us, because we are yours. Turn your gaze downward. *Respice*, it says in Latin: bend down, as a mother bends down, and make us feel your closeness. Make it perceptible as a tangible reality—*sentiamus effectum*, it says in Latin—so that your mercy does not remain merely a word that we hear about, while the reality is something else, but rather so that we can perceive it, that it might become an experience among us. This is the prayer of the Church on this day. Let us urgently entrust it to God's heart on behalf of all the suffering people of this world.

But the Church adds something else, too; she, so to speak, points us to the place where God bends down, so that we can perceive the magnetic field of his closeness. Indeed, we read: "so that we might experience the reality of your mercy, grant that we may be able to serve you wholeheartedly." God's glance is perceived wherever the heart is single, not divided between words for God and actions for ourselves, where it is undivided and makes itself entirely available to God: that is where God is close to us, and that is where we can recognize that he is not an empty, consoling word, but a reality that enters into our lives.

And, therefore, let us pray to him also that we will let him urge us once again to have an undivided, single heart that is entrusted to him and turned toward him; and so that in this turning to the Lord, in this readiness to welcome him and serve him, we may recognize and experience the truth of his mercies, the truth of redemption.

# THE SIGN OF MARY

*Is 7:1–17; Lk 1:26–45*

" 'Ask a sign of the LORD your God.' . . . 'I will not ask, and I will not put the LORD to the test' " (Is 7:11–12).

The response that King Ahaz gives to the prophet Isaiah seems, at first glance, to be an answer informed by faith, indeed, by a mature, disinterested faith, animated by an acute sense of God's transcendence with respect to the historical vicissitudes of the chosen people. To ask the Lord for a sign may mean to put him to the test, as the Hebrews in the desert put him to the test several times by doubting. Is true faith not the faith that needs no signs, the faith that "believes without seeing", as the Risen Jesus will say to Thomas? Is it not contrary to the purity of faith in the God of the Universe to involve him in the political questions of a particular nation, to make him a party in a little war among little kings? In those days, indeed, the kingdom of Judah was attacked jointly by the armies of two neighboring peoples: the army of Rezin, King of Syria, and that of Pekah, King of Israel. The fear of this attack was so great that "[the king's] heart and the heart of his people shook as the trees of the forest shake before the wind" (Is 7:2). Confronted with these threats, King Ahaz thinks about asking Assyria for help. His plan is in keeping with the logic of political realism: this alliance now appears to be the last resort that can ensure the survival of the kingdom of Judah against the aggressors.

However, in contrast to this "politics of reason", the prophet Isaiah proposes the "politics of faith": the historical durability of the people of Israel is dependent, not on human alliances, but on faith in the Lord. Therefore, he admonishes King Ahaz not to ally himself with Assyria and to trust in Yahweh alone. If God has chosen Israel, has established it as his people, and has given it his promises, then only God can save it in a time of danger.

In contrast to Isaiah's position, the "realist" attitude of Ahaz is then revealed for what it is deep down: a lack of faith. Of course, in the abstract, Ahaz does not deny the existence of God; on the contrary, he seems to defend God's absolute transcendence over concrete political events. In reality, what Ahaz denies is that God can intervene in history, that faith in him can have a concrete relevance in the web of events that affect the life of nations and of individual persons. In response to this radical and practical lack of faith, God himself intervenes to give a sign, that is, to cause within history a concrete event that shows his salvific presence. "Behold, a virgin shall conceive and bear a son, and shall call his name Immanuel" (Is 7:14). Immanuel means "God-with-us", God in the midst of his people, concrete company within the events of history.

In the midst of history, which is made up of the wars of the powerful and their intrigues, their attempts to make peace and form alliances, behold: the Lord himself causes a new event, a new story. Faith is not foreign to history. On the contrary, it is able to recognize in history the sign of God's presence, and thus within history it generates a new story.

The Church has always recognized the event of the Annunciation to Mary as the fulfillment of the ancient and mysterious prophecy made by the prophet Isaiah to King

Ahaz. "Do not be afraid, Mary, for you have found favor
with God. And behold, you will conceive in your womb
and bear a son, and you shall call his name Jesus" (Lk 1:30–
31; cf. Is 7:14).

The unbelief of King Ahaz, who refuses the sign, now
corresponds finally to the faith of Mary, who accepts the
sign that is given to her—also the particular sign that
the angel offers her as a help for her faith: the exceptional
motherhood of Elizabeth, who in her old age conceives
a son. Thus, Mary's faith becomes the good, blessed, and
grace-filled soil that welcomes the presence of the Lord
in history, the space that allows him to enter into history.
Through Mary's Yes, through her act of faith, begins
the new story—the story of "God-with-us"—prophesied
by Isaiah.

"The Father of mercies willed that the incarnation
should be preceded by the acceptance of her who was
predestined to be the mother" (*Lumen gentium*, no. 56).
And so, as Augustine said, Mary's conceiving in the spirit,
through faith, preceded her conceiving in the flesh. This
*fiat* of Mary—"let it be to me according to your word"—
decided from the human perspective the fulfillment of
the divine mystery. This harmonizes fully with the words
of the Son, who, according to the Letter to the Hebrews,
upon entering the world says to the Father: "Sacrifices
and offerings you have not desired, but a body have you
prepared for me.... 'Behold, I have come to do your
will, O God'" (Heb 10:5, 7). The Incarnation of Immanuel, of "God-with-us", is possible through this harmony
of the creatures' Yes, of Mary's Yes, with the Yes of
the Son. We could say that Mary's greatness lies, not in
having become Mother of God, because that is God's
greatness, but in having said Yes to the great encounter
that touched her heart.

Mary's faith is therefore the space opened up so that God may enter into history and generate a new story within the uncertain, confusing web of historical events.

Because of her faith, Mary is blessed. "Blessed is she who believed" (Lk 1:45). "All generations will call me blessed" (Lk 1:48). And, nevertheless, Mary's faith, like all genuine faith, is constantly marked by trials, by concealment, by the dimension of the Cross.

The angel had announced to her: "He will be great, and will be called the Son of the Most High; and the Lord God will give to him the throne of his father David, and he will reign over the house of Jacob for ever; and of his kingdom there will be no end" (Lk 1:32–33). No sooner has the mystery of God taken flesh in her than suddenly she is left alone: "And the angel departed from her" (Lk 1:38). How trying it would be to keep this mysterious secret by herself (a mystery totally entrusted to her, a girl from an isolated village in Galilee)! And what a trial it would be for her to keep faith in the One who "will be called Son of God and will reign forever", while her Son Jesus during the thirty years of his hidden life was considered by everyone to be merely the humble son of the carpenter? Especially in the most intimate proximity with Jesus in their daily life in Nazareth, the Mystery remains for Mary truly a Mystery. And she can reach it only through faith. But especially beneath the Cross, where everything seems to be finished forever, even Mary's faith goes through its supreme trial, through total darkness. "A sword will pierce through your own soul also" (Lk 2:35). Thus Mary remains for us forever not only an example of how in faith a human creature opens up space for the Lord's presence, but also the perfect image of what it means "to walk by faith" through everyday life and its trials while keeping and increasing in oneself the light of faith, the memory of God who is mysteriously present beside us.

The announcement of the Marian Year that the Holy Father has proclaimed reaches us, too, in the concrete history through which we are living, on this eve of the third millennium of the Incarnation of the Lord.

Much more than in the days of King Ahaz, facing the events that mark the present moment, we are tempted by bewilderment, and our hearts "shake as the trees of the forest shake before the wind". Not only do we observe the threats of external enemies; the very progress achieved by man seems to ensnare mankind. We sometimes get the impression of having created mechanisms of scientific development, systems of information and control, constructive and destructive energies, which are at the same time stupendous and terrifying, which slip out of our hands and endanger us. A sense of helplessness and mistrust sometimes seems to take possession of mankind, bitterly replacing the euphoria of progress that characterized the era immediately preceding ours.

Given this discouragement, the disappointments resulting from the hopes placed in the presumed realism of world politics, big questions arise once again in our hearts: What is true progress? What is the meaning of history? How can we preserve and defend life? To us also today the prophet says: "Seek a sign from the Lord your God."

The Marian Year that we are experiencing is the great appeal made to us to recognize the sign that has already been given to us. "Behold, a virgin shall conceive and bear a son, and shall call his name Immanuel", "God-with-us".

The sign of Mary, on the eve of the third millennium, shows us the way of genuine human progress.

The sign of Mary is above all the sign of the fruitfulness of faith in history.

The psychoanalyst Erich Fromm, who died a few years ago, radicalized the distinction formulated by Gabriel Marcel between being and having in the alternative: "to be or to have". He pointed out the sickness of our Western civilization in the fact that we transform everything into "having". But one can have something only if it has been reduced first to something inert, something dead. Therefore, he described our civilization, which is a civilization of having, also as a civilization of necrophilia, of love for dead things and for death. Perhaps in saying that, he was too radical. However, it is quite right to say that mere progress in having turns by an intrinsic logic into progress toward death. Progress in having that is not accompanied by progress in being is lethal. But we can achieve progress in being only through an interior deepening, through contemplation, in which we open ourselves to true meaning and thus become assimilated to it, becoming likewise full of meaning ourselves. A civilization without contemplation cannot last long.

Moreover, a Christian community without contemplation cannot last long. A Christianity that is too much conditioned by the Western activist mentality, in which everything depends on doing, on planning, placing trust in one's own resources, a Christianity that increasingly separates Christ from his Mother, little by little sees its own spiritual roots wither. We wonder whether this will lead to what Louis Marie de Montfort observes in comments on the prophet Haggai (1:6): " 'You do much, but nothing comes of it.' If making gains the upper hand and becomes autonomous, the things that we cannot make but are alive and need to mature will no longer survive."

The Marian Year invites us to look to Mary, to understand her faith, her readiness, her contemplation as the space where life is welcomed and can mature.

In this Marian Year, the sign of Mary is shown to us not only as an example but also as a Mother who really cooperates today in the flourishing of the Church's life. If the Church in her everyday dimension does not want to be reduced merely to an arid institution and to exhausting activism, she must look to her. Life can grow and develop only beneath the warmth of a maternal heart.

She, Mary, who in faith gave Christ—life—to the world, continues today with her maternal intercession to generate in the world, through our faith, the Church as a concrete space of life and hope within human history.

# THE FAIR, GOOD HEART OF MARY

*Sir 24; Ps 45; Lk 11:27–28*

In the prayer of today's Marian Mass, we ask the Lord to save us "from the evils that now sadden us". It becomes easy to make this prayer of the Church our own and to bring it before the Lord from the depths of our hearts as our personal prayer. "The evils that now sadden us": we think about the wars, all the acts of violence that devastate the world. We think about the millions of people who suffer from hunger. We think about the families that are torn apart and destroyed. We think about the many people of the world who are without God and without faith, whose life is so empty and devoid of meaning that they seek refuge in drugs or in other forms of stupefaction or adhere to ideologies of violence and drag others, too, into their misfortune. But we think also about the sufferings of pious believers who are sorely tried. We think about the difficulties of the Church herself: the profound divisions and rifts within the Church that obscure her face; in catechesis and the study of theology, young people do not find the nourishment they need; the shortage of vocations in a time when priests and religious are so much needed; the loneliness of many priests, young and old, who find themselves exposed to mockery or to criticism precisely because of their fidelity.

"Save us from the evils that now sadden us!" We know that this prayer of ours does not fall into a vacuum. We

know that our God is a God who listens and sees, who
loves and works. He stretches out his hand toward us to
draw us out of the difficulties of our time. The Reading
and the Gospel today are, so to speak, the outstretched
hand of God who comes in response to our prayer. With
the holy strength of his Word, the Lord wants to draw us
out of the evils and to bring us to joy. The Gospel says:
"Blessed . . . are those who hear the word of God and keep
it!" (Lk 11:28). Behind these words stands the figure of
Mary as she is described in the first chapters of the Gospel of Luke. Mary is the woman who listens attentively,
who is completely open interiorly to the gentle calls of the
Lord. The words of the psalm with which Saint Benedict
starts his *Rule* come to mind: "Hear, O daughter, consider,
and incline your ear" (Ps 45:10). Mary is the daughter of
the king who is all ears, completely open to the message
of joy that comes to her from the Lord: "Rejoice, O full of
grace: the Lord is with you!" (cf. Lk 1:28).

"The king will desire your beauty" (Ps 45:11). Someone who is called by God is touched by joy, because God
is love and, for this reason, joy comes from him. Into the
sadness of time falls the light of eternal love: "The king
will desire your beauty." We are not left alone; we are
not forgotten; we are not empty and without meaning in
the world. God knows us and loves us. The *Rule of Saint
Benedict* as a whole is like a comment on the psalm verse
with which it starts. The *Rule* teaches us to be vigilant for
the call of the King who turns to us. It introduces us to
a Marian way of life. Part of listening is keeping. Three
times in the Gospel about the infancy of Jesus, Luke tells
us that Mary kept these words and meditated on them in
her heart (Lk 1:29; 2:19, 51). Thus, in Mary is fulfilled
the parable of the grain of wheat and the good ground:
"And as for [the seed] in the good soil, they are those

who, hearing the word, hold it fast in an honest and good heart, and bring forth fruit with patience" (Lk 8:15). The word needs a "fair and good heart", as it says literally in the original Greek. It needs to be kept, and, in order to mature, it needs our perseverance, our patience. Momentary enthusiasm is not enough. The great moment of one's first encounter with the Lord can become fruitful only if with great humility and patience we persevere even in times of aridity. That is how plentiful fruit grows. After the unforgettable moment of the Annunciation, "the angel departed from [Mary]" (Lk 1:38). Following the birth of the Lord is the flight into Egypt; then come the long, silent years of the hidden life of Jesus, in which he just seems to be like everyone else, years in which nothing happens outwardly. These are followed by the years of Jesus' public life, which were so difficult for Mary, during which she has to watch the growing hostility toward him yet can do nothing about it. Through these years the words apply: "O woman, what have you to do with me? My hour has not yet come" (Jn 2:4). She must step back and leave the Lord free for his mission.

Then follows the Cross. The "hour" of the Lord has arrived; his exaltation occurs in the sign of suffering. And once again Mary remains hidden. She will appear only in the Scriptures that came into being after her departure from this world. In order for the fruit to grow, this patience is necessary. To become Marian and Benedictine means: to enter into the Marian patience of maturation. Where it is lacking, there is no fruit. The splendor of Jesus' promise: "blessed are they..." illuminates our entire path. But it can break into our life definitively if it includes not only listening but also keeping the word in a fair and good heart.

Now we must take at least a short look at the Reading from the Wisdom Books. Here the one speaking is the mysterious figure of created wisdom, not the Eternal Logos himself, as Athanasius correctly emphasized. But who or what is this created wisdom? About it the text says: "In the holy tabernacle I ministered before him, and so I was established in Zion" (Sir 24:10). Consequently, created wisdom is above all adoration; it is the service of glorifying God present in time. This is again reechoed in Psalm 45, this time in verse 1, which we recite in the Introit: "My heart overflows with a goodly theme." According to the view of the Old Testament teacher of wisdom, created wisdom coincides in fact with the Torah, the holy Law of God, in which God's eternal designs are transformed into ordinances for human life. The center of these ordinances is the temple, the holy tent that God prepared for himself on Mount Zion as a place for the encounter between God and man.

But the temple made of stone was only a shadow, as the Fathers of the Church tell us based on the message of the New Testament: Mary became the true Zion, the sacred tent in which God was able to take up residence corporeally. She made herself available, soul and body, so that the Son of God could take flesh. The whole Torah is now concentrated in the humble and great words that are the summary of all wisdom: "Behold, I am the handmaid of the Lord; let it be to me according to your word" (Lk 1:38). Saint Benedict formulates in his own way the center of wisdom when he says: "Nihil operi Dei praeponatur," (Let nothing be preferred to the Work of God [divine worship]) (*Rule of Saint Benedict*, 43, 3).

From adoration the light of God's presence repeatedly descends anew upon our days. In the Holy Eucharist, the Lord not only speaks with us; with his sacred Body he remains in the midst of us and is united to us, so that we might become "one spirit with him" (1 Cor 6:17). In the

Holy Mass, the eternal Sabbath—the freedom of the children of God—enters into our world. And so, in conclusion, we have arrived once more at the prayer from which we started. Now we can understand it more deeply and pray even better. We spoke about the difficulties of our time and mentioned some of them. All these sad misfortunes have their root in the very nature of time: time is transience. Time, in a world marked by sin, is essentially time toward death. It is determined by death. But death, in which there is no splendor of eternity, is sadness itself: the end of all joy. Only the victory over death can ultimately overcome the sadness of time, too. In the prayer, we ask for "health of mind and body". Missing from the translation is an important word of the Latin text, though: the prayer is for "perpetua mentis et corporis sanitas". *Perpetua* is more than the "always" in the translation. By no means do we want to gloss over the very human intention of this prayer. We pray for health of body and mind because we know that basically the two things are inseparable. And we do so with great trust in God's goodness, because salvation is a great gift. But the prayer, based on the Church's faith, is much bolder. It prays for the "eternal health" of the body, too: this means that we pray for the resurrection! We pray for eternal life. And we can pray for this, with the assurance of being lifted up as the Lord has promised us, if we pray "in his name" (Jn 14:13): only at this point is the sadness of time broken; only in this way does true joy luminously break into our lives.

Behind these words appears once again the figure of Mary. After the Resurrection of the Lord, she was the first to be assumed soul and body into heaven, in other words, into communion with God One and Triune. To her was given eternal health of body and soul. In her, this prayer was heard, because she listened to the Word of God and kept it in a good heart; because with soul and body she made herself available to the Word of God, thus being the fertile ground from which the New Adam could be shaped.

She not only listened; she also responded. With her whole life she became a "love song" to the Lord (Ps 45, inscription). Let us pray to her, the Blessed Virgin and Mother, that she may help us to become a dwelling place for the Lord, so that in this way the light of joy might come from God to illuminate our lives thoroughly.

# BELIEVE, AND YOU WILL SEE ...

*Jn 2:1–11*

The Lord donated about six hundred liters of choice wine for the guests at the wedding in Cana, transforming the water that the servants had drawn, following his instructions. Even if we consider that Eastern weddings lasted a whole week and brought together the entire extended families of the spouses, this is still an inconceivable abundance. Abundance—superabundance—is God's mark on his creation. He squanders the entire universe to make room for man. He gives life in inconceivable abundance. And in the redemption, he squanders himself and becomes man, taking on all the poverty of the human condition, because nothing is enough to show his love. Superabundance is the expression of a love that neither keeps score nor calculates but gives unselfishly. The superabundance of Cana aligns with God's way of revealing himself to mankind throughout the course of history. He gives us a glimpse of the magnificence, grandeur, and inexhaustible goodness of God.

Alongside the miracle of the wine in the Gospel is the miracle of the bread (Jn 6:1–13), in which the Lord satisfies thousands of people with five loaves, providing so much that twelve baskets full of bread are left over. If the bread is the symbolic image of what man needs to live, the wine is already by itself the symbolic image of superabundance, which we also need. It is a sign of joy and of the transfiguration of creation. It draws us out of the sadness and fatigue of daily life and turns being together into a celebration. It expands the senses and the soul, loosens the tongue and opens the heart; it moves us a little beyond the barriers that define our existence.

In this way, wine has become the symbolic image of the gift of the Holy Spirit: tradition speaks of the "sober inebriation" that the Spirit gives, evidently taking its cue from the account of the Pentecost in which the apostles seem to the onlookers to be drunkards (see Acts 2:13). They were sober and inebriated at the same time: they were filled with the joy of the Holy Spirit, who had thrown life wide open to them, who inspired their words, which did not come from themselves, and enabled them to perceive the beauty of a life illumined by the light of the living God.

In this way, we begin to understand something of the meaning of this miracle of the wine that John explicitly describes as a "sign" (Jn 2:11), therefore as a reality that points to something greater beyond what immediately occurred. The greatness of the gift suggests how inexhaustible God's love is, speaks of a love that comes from the Eternal, which is immeasurable and therefore redeeming. The miracle of the wine helps us to understand what it means to receive the Holy Spirit through Christ in faith: a new height and a new fullness of life.

But we have to take another step: we said that the wine creates festivity. In fact, in this Gospel, it is associated with a wedding feast (see Jn 2:1). The wine points to the greatness of what happens in that event, namely, the fact that two people become one through the love instilled in them by the Creator, which makes them become "one flesh" (Gen 2:24), just as Adam says at the dawn of creation, according to the biblical account, when

God leads the woman to him and only thereby makes his life complete.

In this way, however, the sign at Cana points to something even deeper: Jesus came to lead human nature—man himself—to spousal communion with God. God and his creature must be one: not "one flesh" but "one spirit", as Paul says (1 Cor 6:17). Paul puts it this way, too: believers, together with Christ, will be one body—his body (see 1 Cor 12:27). Finally, with the Incarnation in Mary's womb, this wedding has already occurred: God, the Son of God, has taken on human flesh, the very being of man, so that the true man Jesus and the eternal Son of God together form one single person. This wedding, which occurred in the mystery of the Incarnation, must now be extended to all of history. The Lord wishes to embrace, "to draw all men to himself" (see Jn 12:32), so that in the end "God may be everything to every one" (1 Cor 15:28).

Jesus' "hour", which he himself mentions in response to his Mother (Jn 2:4), is the hour of the wedding. He moves toward this hour; he is here for this. It begins, as we said, with his conception in his Mother's womb and reaches its summit on the Cross, which John at the same time always describes as the moment of Jesus' "glorification". On the Cross, he gives himself completely. The Cross is the act by which he gives himself to mankind completely and definitively and thus draws together and holds all of us in his arms. Since this is the final and highest degree of love, the hour of glorification is spent in utter humiliation. Never did God's love become so powerfully visible as in the moment when the Son loved us "to the end" (Jn 13:1). From the pierced side of Jesus came forth "blood and water" (Jn 19:34): Baptism and the Eucharist. The two fundamental sacraments of the Church spring from here. The Eucharist is the definitive gift of new wine in such superabundance and fullness as to last for all ages and all generations. The gift of wine at Cana foreshadows this wine as Jesus' true gift of love, as the real manifestation of his divine glory among us.

At the end of the Cana narrative, there is a phrase by which the Evangelist reveals the meaning of this episode: Jesus "manifested his glory; and his disciples believed in him" (Jn 2:11). The true purpose of the episode at Cana was not the wine, which is only "a sign" consumed and long since gone. The purpose was to manifest Jesus' glory, to make God's infinite goodness shine and, thus, to awaken faith in the disciples. The deeper miracle of Cana is the faith of the disciples, who begin to look beyond the external event and to recognize the greater reality: God's holy presence among us.

Even today, this is what it is about; and from this perspective we understand Mary's mission, which emerges in the account of the wedding. Mary does not ask the Lord to perform a miracle (it was not yet clear at all whether performing miracles was part of his mission); she simply presents to the Lord the difficult situation in which their friends found themselves. She puts everything into Jesus' hands and lets him decide what to do. Even his apparent refusal does not discourage her. Her trust in Jesus, her son, and her union with his will (which is still unknown to her) remain firm. Mary already speaks to us here: again and again we, too, must face certain refusals in our relationship with the Lord: "For my thoughts are not your thoughts" (Is 55:8). We experience the truth of these words from the Bible in our lives. It is therefore important to set aside our obstinacy and not to give in to disappointment or even to doubt. In just this way, we can learn to allow our often mistaken will to be transformed, so that it becomes conformed to God's will and, therefore, upright.

Mary's words to the servants then follow. After her *fiat*, they are perhaps her most beautiful words. Basically, they are only the application of that *fiat*—of her Yes—to all of us and for all of us: "Do whatever he tells you" (Jn 2:5). For us this means: put your will into his will. Be listening and ready to respond to his call. Consider him as the Lord who shows the way and leads us in the right way. With these words, Mary invites the servants and us to have faith. She did not ask for the miracle of the wine as such but, rather, left entirely open-ended what the Lord would do. But she issued a call to faith, thereby leading to the true miracle. Elizabeth greeted Mary, who had come to visit her, with these words: "Blessed is she who believed" (Lk 1:45). With her faith, Mary opened the door to the Incarnation of the Word, to the holy wedding between the eternal God and his creature, man. On the basis of her own faith, she becomes a guide to the faith—*Hodegetria* [she who points the way], as the Eastern Church says— in the bridal mystery of love. In this way, Mary anticipated the core of the event at Cana and shows us what matters, what lasts forever.

"Do whatever he tells you": believe in Jesus Christ, the Son of the living God. Believe with a faith that is love; believe with a faith that is not merely theoretical but alive. Believe with a faith that accepts God's will, even though we do not understand it and even though it is contrary to our will. Believe, and then in the midst of earthly things you will see God's glory, the superabundance and splendor of his love. Believe, and you will see: where others see only the Cross, failure, and a disgraceful end, you will see the immensity of God's extravagant love, his glory that saves us. Believe—then you will receive the choice wine of God's presence in your life. Believe, and the miserable water of our daily routine and the paltry offerings that we can bring will be transformed into the wine of his holy intimacy.

Mary speaks to us this way, right here in Fatima. At the foot of the Cross, the Lord made her the mother of the disciple whom he loved (see Jn 19:26–27). This is why she can no longer vanish from history. This is why she is here with him and for him. This is why she speaks to us even today. Through the two great signs of Lourdes and Fatima, Mary is among us and addresses us. There is no need for many words, because this essential phrase says it all: "Do whatever he tells you." Mary spoke to the little ones, to the unsophisticated, in the midst of an enlightened world that is filled with pride of knowledge and faith in progress, but also filled with destruction, fear, and despair: "They have no wine" (Jn 2:3), only water. How true this is today! Mary speaks to the unsophisticated to show us what matters, the one thing that is necessary, the simplest thing that is equally important for all and equally possible for all: believing in Jesus Christ, the blessed fruit of her womb. We thank her for her maternal presence, for the fact that she speaks to us vividly and powerfully in this place. And we ask her: "After this our exile, show unto us ... Jesus. O clement, O loving, O sweet Virgin Mary!"

# ALL SAINTS: THE FEAST THAT
# DRIVES AWAY DESPAIR

*Is 49:16*

We are celebrating the Solemnity of All Saints. Today in the celebration of the Eucharist, we pray: "Almighty ever-living God, by whose gift we venerate in one celebration the merits of all the Saints, bestow on us, we pray, through the prayers of so many intercessors, an abundance of the reconciliation with you for which we earnestly long." Our gaze therefore turns to the many souls who have preceded us marked with the sign of faith. They are our brothers and sisters, *we* are their brothers and sisters, members of the one big family of God that embraces all time and space. The guide and center of this family is our brother, Jesus Christ. In this family, some names stand out and are well known to all. They are the great saints, witnesses to the power of grace and to the faith that conquers all. They are, however, only the tip of the iceberg. Most of them are unknown. This says nothing about their journey, their life, their witness, or their grace before God and men. To us they are nameless, unknown, just as we, too, will be one day. But not to God. This is precisely what makes them saints: the fact that God knows them and that these magnificent words apply to a high degree to them: "I have graven you on the palms of my hands [i.e., you belong to me]" (Is 49:16). All the members of this family of God are related: God has called them, as he has also called us. God has acted in such a way that they have listened. He bends down to his family with love and mercy. He gathers them all in faith, hope, and love.

But why can we say and pray "Bestow on us *through the prayers of so many intercessors*"? Is it not almost self-evident that the saintly brothers and sisters in our family look upon us with God's loving gaze? What moved their hearts when they had to complete their pilgrimage, in other words, love in imitating Christ, is not something past and finished. On the contrary: only now, face to face with the living God, does all this acquire its definitive form of goodness. Indeed, "love never ends" (1 Cor 13:8). So now they intercede for us. And for this reason, we call them our "intercessors"; interceding, as the prayer says, so that we may receive the blessings "for which we earnestly long".

The Solemnity of All Saints is, in the deepest sense, a celebration of our hope. This, however, makes several demands on us. Christians are people who affirm the reality of God and count on it. This is what it means to believe. Likewise, it can be affirmed with good reason that Christians are people who accept God's promises, build on them, and rely on them. In other words, they hope. Hope is the other side of the coin of faith. In a man's life, however, there can be a disconnect between the two sides. Someone can say "I believe", and yet have very little hope. He is full of disappointment. He once lived joyfully, was expectant, as we say about mothers, that is, with many great expectations about life. One or another of these might have been fulfilled, in fact, would surely have been fulfilled—let us not be ungrateful! How could someone live without hope and without even the slightest spiritual fulfillment? How could anyone continue to live without this kind of experience? And nonetheless, the creeping illness of our time is called hopelessness. It seems to take root everywhere. Ask the elderly. It was once said of them that they were the wisest of all people, rich with great experience in life; and for this reason, they were honored and accepted by everyone. Today, instead, among these very same people, are there not many who are hopeless and no longer expect anything? But why? Because they are left alone. They seem to be forgotten. They often seem to be "left over" from a past world, and no one knows quite what to do with them. There is no need for them. An old man who dragged himself around like a forgotten soul once said: "No one is expecting me." There it is: this was his deep sadness, his hopelessness.

But is this true? Is there really no one who expects him? It may be true in relations with others and in the relations of some people toward others. The reality, though, is greater and far surpasses what we immediately see and experience. Beneath the surface of today's feast, a powerful cry is perceptible: "You are expected!" Definitively and forever, with the guarantee that your expectations will be fulfilled. Finally, after perhaps having carried some burdens for a long time and having asked yourself whether it all had any meaning. The cry of hope and encouragement from the finish line reaches those who are still on the journey. It is a cry made up of many voices, a cry that causes hope to dawn. Not in emptiness, no. Hoping with assurance and trust, hoping in a community and in a brotherhood that knows no disturbance, because the one calling is God, who alone makes all other voices possible. "The God of our faith is the foundation of our hope." "Our hope is Jesus Christ."[1] What was said in the passage cited a little earlier? "I have graven you on

[1] Joint Synod of the German Dioceses.

the palms of my hands" (Is 49:16). In light of the feast that we celebrate and in the light of so many testimonies, we can only say: "In you, Lord, is our hope, and we shall never hope in vain" (*Te Deum*).

# SOURCES

## ADVENT AND THE CHRISTMAS SEASON

*Someone Who Has Found Love Can Say: I Have Found Life*
Homily given on December 3, 1987, for the Community of Don Orione, Rome.

*Only Love Knows Love*
Homily given on December 8, 1989, Solemnity of the Immaculate Conception of the B.V.M., on the occasion of a meeting in Castel Gandolfo with the Focolari Movement of Rocco di Papa (Rome).

*How God Comforts*
Homily given on December 10, 1978, in the parish of Sankt Martin in Unterwössen, Germany.

*God's Weeping and the Promise of Victory*
Homily given on December 12, 2003, for the Centro internazionale giovanile di San Lorenzo [Saint Lawrence International Youth Center].

*Mary's Yes: "Blessed Is She Who Believed"*
Homily given on December 18, 1988, at a convent in Rome on the Fourth Sunday of Advent.

*Plunging into God's Love*
Homily given on December 25, 1979, at the Cathedral in Munich.

# LENT AND THE EASTER SEASON

*The Celebration of Lent*
Homily given on February 20, 1980, at Saint Boniface Abbey in Munich.

*"Behold Your Mother!" These Words Are Addressed to Us, Too*
Homily given on April 11, 1987, at the International Seminary in Rome.

*Joseph's Faith*
Homily given on March 18, 1984, in Saint Joseph parish.

*"Do with Me What You Will, Only Grant That I May Love You Completely"*
Homily for Holy Thursday, given in Munich on April 12, 1979.

*When God Kneels Down before Us*
Homily for Holy Saturday, given in the Cathedral in Munich on April 3, 1980.

*"I Have Risen, and Now I Am Always with You"*
Homily for Easter Sunday, given in Wigratzbad, Germany, on April 15, 1990.

# ORDINARY TIME

*"Blessed Are You When Men Hate You"*
Homily given on February 15, 1998, at the Church of Saint Jerome of the Croats, Rome.

*When a Machine Is Blessed*
Visit on April 26, 1986, to Montecastrilli (Province of Terni, Italy) to bless the tractors.

*"Only He Who Experiences the Absurd Is Able to Conquer the Impossible" (Miguel de Unamuno)*
Homily given on May 19, 1992, at the Church of the Holy Apostles in Rome.

*On the Way to the Land of the Future*
Homily given on June 5, 1980, at Marienplatz in Munich.

*Jesus and the Faith of the Little Ones*
Meditation given in Münster on September 6, 1970.

*The Genuine Miracle Is God Crucified*
Meditation given in Münster on September 7, 1970.

*The Main Thing Needed to Purify the Empoisoned Air of This World*
Homily given on July 24, 2001, in Fontgombault, France.

*The Cross: The Love That Gives Itself, Total Self-Giving to Others*
Homily given on September 15, 1979, in Munich.

*The Sign of Mary*
Homily given on September 17, 1988, on the occasion of the Feast of the Stigmata of Saint Francis, Shrine of La Verna (Province of Arezzo, Italy).

*The Fair, Good Heart of Mary*
Homily given on September 23, 1995, in Le Barroux, France.

*Believe, and You Will See* ...
Homily given on October 13, 1996, in Fatima.

*All Saints: The Feast That Drives Away Despair*
Homily given for the Solemnity of All Saints (no date).

# INDEX

Abel, 98, 100–101
Abraham, 52, 53, 96–100, 122
Adam, 9, 12, 142–43
Advent: expectation of,
    23–30; God's comfort and,
    18–22; guidance of Mary,
    31–34, 151; Immaculate
    Conception, 14–17; Mount
    of Olives and, 61–62;
    watchfulness and, 23–24
Ahaz, King of Judah, 128–30,
    132
All Saints, Solemnity of,
    147–50, 154
Ambrose of Milan, Saint, 25, 81
Amos the prophet, 18
angels, 32, 74, 126, 130. *See also*
    Gabriel, Archangel
*Apology* (Plato), 80
Archelaus, King of Judea, 55
Archimedes, 116
Ash Wednesday, 43
Assyria, 128, 129
Athanasius, Saint, 138
Augustine of Hippo, Saint, 25,
    50, 83, 130
Augustus, Emperor of Rome,
    55, 125

Babylonian Exile, 18, 27
Baptism, 9, 60, 143
beatitudes, 79–80, 81–82
Benedict of Nursia, Saint, 43,
    45, 66, 136, 138

Bethlehem, 36
blessings, 79–80, 81–82, 86–88,
    137
Blood of Christ, as gift, 48–49
Bonaventure, Saint, 25
bread: as gift, 30, 87–88, 121;
    miracle of the, 141; offered
    by Abraham, 122; offered
    by Melchizedek, 99
Brecht, Bertolt, 20

Cain, 100–101
Cana, wedding at, 48–49,
    141–46
catholic (term), 39
Celebration of the Forty Days
    (*Quadragesima*), 43–46
charity, 9, 14–15, 32
Charles Borromeo, Saint, 25
chastity, 66, 93
Christian life: essence of, 23,
    48; first communities of,
    29; foundation of, 65; glory
    of God in, 115; human
    need and, 105, 109; Mary
    as perfect model of, 14;
    mutual acceptance in, 97;
    work and, 88
Christianity: heart of, 124;
    meaning of, 9, 10, 38;
    resentment and, 114–16;
    views of, 37
Christmas, 22, 35–40, 151. *See
    also* Incarnation; Nativity

Church: blessings and, 86; as
    body of Christ, 75, 93–94;
    difficulties of, 135; faith and,
    39, 83, 124, 139; foundation
    of, 124; history of as light,
    25; human nature and, 64,
    100, 115, 120; liturgical
    year, 19, 44; Mary and,
    14, 31–32, 47, 49–50, 134;
    obedience to, 19, 93–94,
    113; priests and bishops of,
    74, 135; as sacrament, 94;
    Schlier on, 68; in Spain, 91;
    suspicions against the, 34; on
    work, 88; in Yugoslavia, 84
Claudel, Paul, 64
commandments, 10, 26, 33
Communism, 27, 80
compassion, 21, 47–51
conscience, 18, 80–81
consolation, 18–22
Corinthians, Letter to the,
    16–20, 79–85
Corpus Christi, feast of, 96,
    97–100
courage, 48, 66–68, 70, 84–85,
    91–92, 126
creation: beauty of, 115–16;
    Christmas and, 36–38;
    culture and, 37; faith and,
    55; gifts of, 88, 99; harmony
    of, 10, 87; love and, 25;
    man as God's, 126, 141;
    new creation, 45, 103;
    transfiguration of, 142
Cross of Christ: blessings
    and, 50–51; Church and,
    74; Eucharist and, 124;
    Exaltation of Holy Cross,
    123; as final rift, 113;

following the, 137; as image
    of love, 125–26; Mary and,
    47–48, 74, 131, 146; new
    Jerusalem from, 29; prelude
    to, 109

Dante Alighieri, 79
David, King of Judah, 131
Day of Preparation, 70, 72
death: consolation and, 20–21;
    freedom from, 45; Fromm
    on, 133; human life and,
    9–10, 31; Jesus and, 69, 71;
    victory over, 139
desert imagery, 10, 44, 46, 83,
    128
Deuteronomy, 9–13
The Divine Comedy (Dante),
    79
divine love: Christianity and,
    10; creativity and, 16;
    divine knowledge and, 15;
    grace and, 15, 16–17, 71;
    man and, 10, 26, 47; order
    of, 116–17
divine nature: Divine
    Motherhood of Mary, 32;
    holiness and, 15–16; sharing
    in, 35–36, 38
divine revelation, 113–14
Doctors of the Church, 25.
    See also Ambrose of Milan,
    Saint; Athanasius, Saint;
    Augustine of Hippo, Saint;
    Bonaventure, Saint; John of
    the Cross, Saint; Leo I, Pope
    Saint; Teresa of Ávila, Saint;
    Thérèse of Lisieux, Saint;
    Thomas Aquinas, Saint
Dominic, Saint, 25

*Dominus flevit* (The Lord Wept)
(chapel), 26–27
*Donum vitae* (Instruction on
Respect for Human Life
in its Origin and on the
Dignity of Procreation)
(CDF), 12

Easter Sunday, 69–76, 152
Edith Stein, Saint, 25
egotism, 13, 19, 44, 45, 60, 65
Elijah the prophet, 18, 19
Elizabeth (mother of John the
Baptist), Saint, 32, 130, 145
Ephesians, Letters to the, 14–17
eternal life: faith and seeking
of, 96; feast of, 46; gift of,
122; perpetual prayer for,
139; preparation for, 88;
water of, 83
eternal love, 17, 25, 71 72, 73,
136
eternity, 45, 54, 71, 89, 139
Eucharist: celebration of, 57,
147; centrality of, 94; cost
of the, 124; Eucharistic
Presence, 48, 49, 75, 100,
138; First Eucharistic
Prayer, 98; as gift, 143–44;
Holy Thursday and, 57, 60,
64; Josemaría Escrivá and,
94; love and, 57–60; origin
of, 35, 143; peace and, 99;
Resurrection and, 73, 124;
water at the, 35–36, 40;
work and, 88
Eve, 9, 32
evil: of darkness, 25, 31, 48, 131;
God's victory over, 29, 89;
hope as stronger than, 109;

prayer to save from, 135–36;
struggle between good and,
32; transforming of, 81

faith: Ahaz and, 128;
communication of, 33;
gift of, 29; healing and,
103–7; Jeremiah on, 18,
27; of Joseph, 52–56; as
journey, 24–25; light of, 20;
of Mary, 32–34, 130–32,
145; new form of living the,
28–29; obedience and, 33;
profession of, 124; return
to, 38; trust and, 32 34; as
work of God, 92–93
fasting, 18, 43–46
Fathers of the Church, 39, 54,
138. *See also* Ambrose of
Milan, Saint; Benedict of
Nursia, Saint; Gregory of
Nyssa, Saint; Origen
fear, 9–10, 15, 59, 61–62,
67 68
foreigners, 96, 97, 101
Francis of Assisi, Saint, 25
fraternity, 9–10, 13, 40
freedom: celebration of, 45;
change and, 28; Christmas
and, 40; endowment
with, 40; fear of hindering
of, 26, 32; fundamental
error concerning, 16; of
goodness, 104–5; grace and,
17; love and, 26, 59, 82; in
suffering, 67
Fromm, Erich, 133

Gabriel, Archangel, 32, 33
Galilee, 74, 75, 91, 118, 131

Genesis, 86–88, 96–101,
     118–22
God: back of, 74–75; blessings
     of, 50–51; comfort from,
     18–22; contact with, 45;
     defense of, 80–81; design
     of, 9; existence of, 53–54;
     harmony with, 32; hidden
     presence of, 54–56; His
     response to suffering,
     19; knowledge of, 13,
     15; love and, 15, 119;
     new day created by, 70;
     omnipotence of, 25–26;
     praise of, 89–90; suffering
     of, 25–26; suspicions
     against, 34; turning to,
     126–27; vengeance of,
     112; victory of, 89; will of,
     91, 93–94; as wisdom, 28,
     29–30
Good Friday, 47, 48
Good Samaritan, 118–19
goodness: freedom of, 104–5;
     path of, 26; return to, 38;
     struggle with evil, 32
grace: charity and, 14–15;
     divine love and, 15, 16–17,
     71; finding, 40; freedom
     and, 17; humility and,
     16–17
Gregory of Nyssa, Saint, 74–75

Haggai the prophet, 133
Hebrews, Letter to the, 35–40
Herod, King of Judea, 55, 125
heroic virtue, 93
holy, defined, 15–16
Holy Family, 54
Holy Saturday, 48, 63–68

Holy Spirit: as the Consoler,
     20; gift of, 142; grace as the,
     14; as love, 60–61; in the
     world, 24
Holy Thursday, 48, 57–62, 65,
     67, 152
Holy Week, 47. *See also specific
     days*
honey imagery, 29
hope: gift of, 29; trust in Christ
     and, 85
*Hosanna*, 69
Hosea the prophet, 18, 19
hospitality, 96, 118–22
*How God Comforts*, 18–22, 151
human nature: assumption
     of, 35–36, 38; burden of
     humanity, 21; as common
     foundation, 39; dignity of,
     36
humility: of Christ, 50, 63–65,
     67; Christian meaning of,
     66–68; grace and, 16–17;
     of Mary, 48; path of, 26;
     return to, 38–39
hymns: on consolation, 22; of
     Passiontide, 68

image and likeness of God:
     being in, 15–16; Christ
     child as reflection of, 38–39
immaculate, defined, 15–16
Immaculate Conception of
     Mary, 14
Incarnation, 32, 35–36, 130, 143
Instruction on Respect for
     Human Life in its Origin
     and on the Dignity of
     Procreation (*Donum vitae*)
     (CDF), 12

Isaac, 53, 99
Isaiah, book of, 18–22, 23–30,
    123–27, 128–34, 147–50
Isaiah the prophet, 18, 21,
    128–30
Israel, 128–29; Babylonian
    Exile, 18; commandments
    and, 26; destruction of
    Jerusalem, 27, 29; Isaiah on,
    22; rift with Jesus, 110–17;
    suffering of, 123

Jacob, 53, 131
Jairus' daughter, raising of,
    102–3, 108–9
Jeremiah, book of, 79–85
Jeremiah the prophet, 18, 27
Jerusalem: destruction of, 27,
    28; *Dominus flevit* (chapel),
    26–27; feast in, 75; New
    Jerusalem, 29
Jesus Christ, 121; being in
    union with, 16; birth
    of Church and, 47–48,
    49; blind beggar and,
    90; Church as body of,
    75, 93–94; communion
    with, 65, 75–76; God and
    man as one in, 40; God
    in, 24; humanity of, 109;
    humility of, 50, 63–65, 67;
    institution of the Eucharist,
    35; knowledge of, 102; as
    Lamb of God, 98, 99; love
    of, 100–101; Melchizedek as
    precursor of, 97; at Mount
    of Olives, 27, 59, 61, 126; as
    new day, 70; parables of, 26,
    63; Paschal words of, 72; on
    peace, 26; Psalm 118 and,

69; public life of, 118, 137;
    rejection of, 123; on riches,
    82–83; rift with Israel,
    110–17; rising of, 73–74;
    sanctity and, 91–92; Sermon
    on the Mount, 16, 79; as
    Son of God, 113–14; Spirit
    of, 37; victory of, 45–46;
    vision of, 79; as the Way,
    21; at wedding in Cana,
    48–49, 141–46; as wisdom,
    28, 29–30
John, Gospel of, 35–40, 47–51,
    57–62, 63–68, 141–46
John of the Cross, Saint, 25
John Paul II, Pope Saint, 50,
    60–61, 79–80, 132
John the Baptist, Saint, 21, 26,
    31
John the Evangelist, Saint, 9,
    15, 47–51, 64–65, 89, 92,
    142–44, 146
Josemaría Escrivá, Saint, 89–95
Joseph (husband of Mary),
    Saint, 52–56, 152
Judah, kingdom of, 33, 128. *See
    also* Ahaz, King of Judah;
    Archelaus, King of Judea;
    Herod, King of Judea
justice, 18, 28–29, 53–56, 90,
    92, 98–99, 124

Lamb of God, 98, 99
Last Judgment, 11
Last Supper, 64
Lent: as Celebration of the
    Forty Days (*Quadragesima*),
    43–46; Joseph as Lenten
    saint, 52–56; liturgy of,
    47–51, 152

Leo I, Pope Saint, 36, 37
liberalism, 72–73
life: fundamental gift of, 13;
    grace and, 40; love as,
    10–11; meaning of, 10;
    truth and, 40
light: spread of path of, 29;
    watchfulness and, 23–25;
    Word of God as, 25
listening: of Mary, 136;
    warning on, 27–28, 30
liturgy: ancient customs of,
    35; of Christmas, 39;
    confirmation of, 29–30;
    liturgical reform, 36; Paschal
    liturgy, 47; theology of, 121
loneliness: consolation and,
    20, 21, 126; fear of, 15, 59;
    Mount of Olives and, 61, 62,
    126; of priests, 135; relations
    with others and, 101
Lourdes, 146
love: confidence and, 32;
    consolation and, 20;
    Eucharist and, 57–60; faith
    as, 145; fasting and, 45;
    freedom and, 26, 59; gift
    of, 29; of God, 13; God as,
    15; Jeremiah on, 27; as life,
    10–11; of Trinity, 4, 71;
    unconditional love, 26. See
    also divine love
Luigi Orione, Saint, 12
Luke, Gospel of, 14–17, 31–34,
    79–85, 89–95, 118–22,
    128–34, 135–40
Luke the Apostle, Saint, 29, 118
Lumen gentium (Vatican II), 130

machines, blessing of, 86–88
Magi, 39

Marcel, Gabriel, 133
marginalization, 103–5
Marian Year, 132, 133–34
Mark, Gospel of, 18–22, 69–76,
    102–9, 110–17
Martha, Saint, 118–22
martyrs, 18, 29
Marx, Karl, 21, 66
Marxism, 72–73, 106
Mary (sister of Martha), Saint,
    118–22
Mary (wife of Clopas), Saint,
    47, 70, 72, 74
Mary, Blessed Virgin, Saint:
    Annunciation, 129,
    137; Assumption of,
    139–40; as blessed, 51,
    131; consecration to, 94;
    contemplation of, 133–34,
    136; Eve and, 32; faith of,
    32–34, 130–32, 145; fiat of,
    31–34, 130, 145, 151; grain
    of wheat parable, 136–37;
    guidance of, 31–32, 48;
    Immaculate Conception of,
    14; Isaiah's prophecy and,
    129–32; mission of, 144; as
    Mother of Church, 47–51;
    Our Lady of Guadalupe,
    94–95; Our Lady of
    Sorrows, 47, 123; as perfect
    model of Christian life, 14,
    16, 17, 136; at the tomb, 70,
    72, 74; at wedding in Cana,
    48–49, 145–46
Mary Magdalene, Saint, 47, 70,
    72, 74
materialism, 72–73
Matthew, Gospel of, 23–30,
    43–46, 52–56
Maximilian Kolbe, Saint, 25

meditation, 54, 79, 119, 120, 136

Melchizedek, 96–100

Micah the prophet, 18

Miracles: Bartimaeus the blind beggar, 90; cycle of, 110; healing of woman, 103–7; Jairus' daughter, raising of, 102–3, 108–9; loaves and fishes, 141; at wedding in Cana, 48–49, 141–46

Montfort, Louis Marie de, 133

moral acts, 65, 119

Mosaic Law, 10–11, 53

Moses, 74

Mount of Olives, 27, 59, 61, 126

Mount Sinai, 26

Nativity: celebration of, 34; feast of the, 31, 36; John Paul II on, 79–80; mystery of, 35 40. *See also* Christmas

Nazareth, 111–14, 117, 131

Nazism, 80

neighbor, love of, 118–22

New Covenant, 100

New Testament: Old Testament becoming, 31; unity with Old Testament, 25, 28, 97; Zion and, 138. *See also specific books*

Nietzsche, Friedrich, 66, 111–14, 117

Noah, 54, 55

obedience, 17, 33, 66, 93–94

Old Covenant, 97, 98, 100

Old Testament: encounter with God in, 97; liturgy of thanksgiving in, 69;

New Testament and, 25, 28, 31, 97; prayer, 55–56, 71; predictions/hopes of, 72; Zion and, 138. *See also specific books*

Opus Dei, 48, 92

Ordinary Time, 79–150, 152–53

Origen, 49

Our Lady of Guadalupe, 94–95

Our Lady of Sorrows, 47, 123

parables, 26, 63, 136–37

Paradise, 9–10, 12

Pascal, Blaise, 61

Passion of the Lord, 47, 60, 79, 94

patience, 48, 52, 137

patriarchs, 52, 53. *See also specific patriarchs*

Paul the Apostle, Saint, 14, 74, 75, 82, 91, 143

peace, 26, 27, 28, 99, 129

Pekah, King of Israel, 128

Penance (sacrament), 60

penance, 43–46

Pentecost, 142

Peter the Apostle, Saint, 50, 91, 92, 124

Pio of Pietrelcina, Saint, 25

Plato, 80

poor people: in beatitudes, 81–82; Jesus as poor, 79–80; love for, 29

praise, 89–90

prayer(s): *Benedictus*, 69; of the Church, 49; for eternal life, 139; intercession of saints, 148; life of, 34; of Mary, 49; *Resurrexi, et adhuc tecum sum* (antiphon), 71; work and, 88

Preparation of the Gifts, 35, 40
pride, 65, 66–67
priesthood, 57, 97. *See also*
    Josemaría Escrivá, Saint
Promised Land, 10
prophets, 18, 19, 26, 31, 33, 52,
    83. *See also specific prophets*
prudence, 54–55
psalms, 26, 29, 69–76, 83, 138

*Quadragesima* (Celebration of
    the Forty Days), 43–46

reconciliation, 81, 112, 117, 147
redemption: in Christian sense,
    21; Holy Spirit and, 61;
    Jesus Christ and, 62; of man,
    36–37; simplicity and, 39
*Redemptor hominis* (John Paul
    II), 60–61
*Redemptoris Mater* (John Paul
    II), 50, 60
renewal, of man, 37–38
repentance, 27, 31
Resurrection: Eucharist and,
    73; Paschal response to,
    69, 76; raising of Jairus'
    daughter and, 102–3, 108–9;
    redemption in, 118; water
    in wine imagery and, 35
*Resurrexi, et adhuc tecum sum*
    (antiphon), 71
Revelation, Book of, 29, 89,
    90
Rezin, King of Syria, 128
righteousness, 18, 55–56
Romans, Letter to the, 89–95

sacrament(s): Church as, 94; of
    conversion, 60; fundamental

sacraments, 143; institution
    of, 59; Jesus as, 60; meaning
    of term, 43–44. *See also*
    *specific sacraments*
sacrifice, 84, 94, 98–99, 101
saints: as catechesis, 52; as
    lights, 25; Solemnity of All
    Saints, 147–50, 154. *See also*
    *specific saints*
salvation: Cross and, 114–15;
    gates of, 69–70; gift of true
    life and, 122; history of, 19,
    98; Holy Family and, 54;
    Israel and, 123; Mary and,
    47; Nativity and, 34
sanctity, 91–92
Schlier, Heinrich, 68
science, 11–12, 72–73
Sermon on the Mount, 16, 79
serpent, 32, 50–51
shepherds, 39
silence, 18, 49, 52, 61, 65, 111,
    137
Simeon, 52
simplicity, 38–39
sin: confession of, 68; fear of,
    37; first sin, 10; Jesus Christ
    and, 69; Mary and, 47;
    Nietzsche on, 114; path of,
    33; Peter on, 92; time and,
    139
Sirach, book of, 135–40
smallness, 91, 114, 116, 117
Socrates, 80
Stepinac, Alojzije Cardinal,
    79–85
suffering: acceptance and,
    45–46, 125–26; comfort
    from, 18–19; freedom
    in, 67; love for suffering

people, 29; of God, 25–26;
  sign of, 137
suspicions, 32, 34

Te Deum, 85, 150
technology, 86–88
Teresa of Ávila, Saint, 25
Teresa of Calcutta, Saint, 25
Thérèse of Lisieux, Saint, 25,
  120–21
Thomas the Apostle, Saint, 128
Thomas Aquinas, Saint, 25
time, 139
Torah, 138
totalitarianism, 80, 81
transcendence, 45, 76, 104,
  109, 128, 129
transformation, 27, 29–30
Trinity, 32, 64, 71, 122, 125
trust, 32–34, 38, 48, 84–85,
  126–27
truth, 29, 40, 66, 67, 80–81, 83

Veritatis splendor (John Paul II),
  79–80

Veronica, Saint, 79
violence, 12, 25, 61, 63,
  100–101, 135

washing of the feet, 59–60,
  63–65, 68, 122
watchfulness, 23–24
water, 35–36, 40, 83–85
wheat imagery, 29–30, 136–37
wine: as gift, 48, 88, 99, 121;
  Melchizedek and, 99;
  mixing water with, 35–36,
  40; at wedding in Cana,
  48–49, 141–46
wisdom, 28–29, 137–38
Word of God: acceptance of,
  53; gift of, 120; guidance of,
  54, 84; Jesus as the, 105–6;
  as light, 25; listening to, 90,
  121; Mary and, 139–40
work, 86–88, 138
World Youth Day, 24–25

Zion, 138